929.4   Lee, Mary Price
LEE
         Your name—all about
         it

DATE DUE

JUN. 2 5 1993			
DEC 0 1 1994			
NOV 1 9 2002 SEP 8 2005			
OCT 1 1 2006			
JAN 3 1			
APR 2 2 2009			
JAN 4 2010			

YOUR NAME—ALL ABOUT IT

WESTMINSTER PRESS BOOKS
by
Mary Price Lee

Your Name—All About It

Ms. Veterinarian

Money and Kids

Your Name–
All About It

By
MARY PRICE LEE

Illustrated by
LEE DeGROOT

THE WESTMINSTER PRESS
Philadelphia

BOOK DESIGN BY DOROTHY ALDEN SMITH

Published by The Westminster Press®
Philadelphia, Pennsylvania
PRINTED IN THE UNITED STATES OF AMERICA
9 8 7 6 5 4 3 2

Library of Congress Cataloging in Publication Data

Lee, Mary Price.
  Your name—all about it.

  Bibliography: p.
  Includes index.
  SUMMARY: Information on the history of names,
changing your name, famous names, nicknames, and
name games. Includes a dictionary of boys' and
girls' names.
    1. Names, Personal—Juvenile literature.
[1. Names, Personal] I. De Groot, Lee.
II. Title.
CS2309.L37   929.4   79-22145
ISBN 0-664-32656-0

To my brother and his family

namely

Bob
Jennifer
Stephen
Colin
and
Teddy

With affection

Mary Price Lee
Mary Lee
Missy Lee
Miss
Mom
"Bee"

CONTENTS

1 *Let's Talk About Your Name*

"Who, me?"

Yes, you! This book is about you—and your name. Your name is full of history. There may be interesting stories about it. If you don't like your name, do you know how to change it? You'll find that names have personality and that names play games. Famous names, odd names, number names, first names around the world, are all explored in these pages. Read on.

What's in a name? Plenty!

Your name is you. It is as unique as your personality, as persistent as your shadow.

Think what life would be like without a name. "Hey, you!" or "Hi, 046213–D" can hardly substitute for "Hey, Barb!" or "Hi, Rick!" Your name is your own personal property. It dresses you up as much as your school clothes do. It is important because you are important.

And who selected your special name? Your parents, most likely. Chances are that long before you made your appearance, someone was sifting through names to arrive at the perfect label for you. The name finally chosen reflects your specialness and separates you from the approximately 2,999,999 other babies born in America during your birth year.

Your name may have been chosen to express your parents' hopes and ideals. Perhaps your name continues a family tradition passed on from generation to generation. Perhaps it reflects daydreams of knights in armor, a heroine in a famous novel, or a favorite doctor. Your name may even have been inspired by a space hero.

The adults in your life may have chosen a name that would say good things about you: "Let's call the baby Timothy. It means Honoring God"; or "If it's a girl, let's call her Monica for Adviser."

Almost all names have meanings. They can express nearly everything from tragedy to sorrow to the state of the weather. Names may include stars, flowers, or colors.

The meaning is often hidden in the change of language from one country to another or by the passage of time, but it is still there. If you are called Susan, you are also Lily, because many years ago Susan meant the flower, lily. Every name has its own definition.

This means that you really have two names. The next time someone asks your name, you can say John, Peter, or Charlotte, or you could answer The Lord Is Gracious, Rock, or Strong, for those are the meanings of the three names. A Vietnamese might say, "My name is Am. It means moonlight."

Of course, it might be awkward to be called by your name's original meaning. What girl wants to be reminded that her name means Loyal if she tends to change friends every week? What boy wants to be called Gracious if he feels like being rude and bratty?

Do you think that if you were called Protector (William or Wilma), you would grow up to be a policeman or policewoman? Would you do better in school if you were on the roll as Divine Wisdom? These names would be pretty tough to live up to.

Some "nice" names do not have pleasant meanings. Who would have guessed that Miriam may mean Bitter? Harvey and Russell are mild-sounding names that are synonyms for Battleworthy and Fox-like.

First names often reflect interests and occupations. If you're a George, farming may be in your future. George is Greek for farmer. A Penelope is bound to do fine needlework because her name means Weaver. In Welsh, Morgan means Sailor. Morgan, familiar as a last name, is used as a first name, too. If your name stands for an occupation, you may want to take a hint and follow your calling.

Animals, insects, and birds also get into the name act. American Indians, Eskimos, and some primitive tribes still use animal names. Asked to think of a historic Indian name, you'll probably come up with Sitting Bull. This doughty Indian chief was the Sioux leader in the Battle of Little Bighorn, in which General Custer and his forces were killed. How do you suppose Sitting Bull got his name? Was it because he was large and strong and looked like a sitting bull? Or did he shoot a sitting bull? Or did he like to sit with sitting bulls?

Actually, legend has it that a reclining bull was the first thing Sitting Bull's father saw after his son was born. American Indians often name a child after an object of nature or a memorable event that occurs during or immediately after birth. Another version is that Sitting Bull's name was Slow until he was fourteen. At that time he went with a war party, fought manfully, and was given the imposing name Sitting Bull. American Indians have other ways of naming their babies which you will read about in Chapter 8.

If your name is Melissa, Debby, or Caleb, you too have a name from nature. Melissa (Bee), Deborah (Bee), and Caleb (Dog) can enjoy their nature-world connections. Their names show the influence that insects and animals once had in the community.

Mythological and classical names are rich in meaning. The ancient Greeks, Romans, and Egyptians enlivened name-giving by using strong adjectives to describe their countrymen. Wise (Sophia), Noble (Eugene), and Faithful (Homer) were apt names for these early empire builders. Many names reflected ancient ideals of wisdom and strength.

However, we have inherited some very warlike names from the fighting gods and goddesses of the ancient world. These gods were very real to the Greeks and Romans, who felt that their daily lives were ruled by them. Mars was Fierce and Fearful, while two-faced Janus was not above deceiving others. The goddess Nemesis was Vengeful and Spiteful. Other gods were so disorderly that their disagreeable names described them well.

Not all the gods were troublemakers. Venus, Zeus, and Juno were among the superhuman citizens whose names translated into good thoughts and deeds.

Many people in the ancient world had names that are popular today. Valerie and Mark, Claire and Martin all go back to civilizations long before Christ. These names and others figure in literary works of that long-ago time.

How do we know the actual meanings of so many names, especially when these meanings are rooted in early history?

The answers come from onomastics, or the study of names. Onomastics has been of interest for many, many years. Scholars have studied old texts to discover the names of ancient people. They have combed tombs and ancient buildings to spot names carved on walls. They have been able to discover the meanings of names by studying the parent languages of those names.

But we do not need to be experts to be curious about names. Everyone is fascinated by them. When a new baby arrives, what are the first two questions? That's right: Is it a boy or a girl? and, What is the baby's name? We are just as interested in the name of the new boy down the street, the new school principal, the new state governor, the new United States President. Once we have a name, we feel as though we have a link to the person.

We also like to know that a name fits. When Pope Paul VI died in 1978, the new pope took the name of John Paul I. He wanted to follow in the footsteps of Pope Paul VI and Pope John XXIII. This was a symbolic move. By combining the names of the two men he admired, he was showing that he wished to be like them. Tragically, he lived only thirty-four days to carry on the role of his predecessors. But the pope that succeeded him also chose the name of John Paul. He became Pope John Paul II. The inspiration of the first John Paul was not to disappear with his death.

When Jomo Kenyatta, president of Kenya, died in August 1978, the world felt that he had lived up to the meaning of his name, Burning Spear. It was indeed an inspiring name for an inspiring person. Kenyatta acted decisively to set his country on a path of progress. His leadership was a burning spear of hope to his countrymen.

Names can be "crowns" for individuals who are loved and respected. Names make people special; people, in turn, make names special.

2 Want to Change Your Name?

Many people are happy with their names. They fit and they flatter and that's what counts. Others would like to rub Aladdin's magic lamp and have the genie come up with a new name.

Are you one of those persons who would like to trade in your name? Do you think it is sissy, sharp-sounding, or ugly? Alben William Barkley, Vice-President under Harry Truman, felt that at the age of sixteen teen-agers should be able to change their name if they didn't like the one their parents gave them. He was originally named Willie Alben.

It is unlikely that Mr. Barkley's idea will ever be adopted, but there is something you can do about a name you don't like. There are ways you can turn it around to come up with something more pleasing. Of course you won't be legally changing your name, but if you want a variation on your present one, here's how to do it.

Take a good look at your middle and last names. Could either of them develop into a name for you? Let's say you are Carl Holbert Judson. You don't like Carl. How about Bert, C.H., or Jud? Or if your name is Susan Elliston Carrington and you don't care for Susan, you have your choice of Ellie or Carrie. Lots of people call their friends by names made up from their middle or last names. Someone whose last name is Bookhammer is bound to be nicknamed Bookie; a MacFarland is almost sure to be Mac. Why not make up just such a nickname for yourself?

Fine, you say, but what about getting people to call you by your new name? It's not easy, but you can do it. You have to train everyone. If you're changing schools or moving, you can easily put your plan into action, because everyone will ask what your name is. Otherwise, you must simply announce that you are

changing your name and plug away at getting the new one accepted.

The start of a new school year is a good time to make the name-change move. Friends will generally go along with you because friends aim to please. The family will remember if you remind them often enough. If people forget, you can always refuse to answer to your old name. Soon enough, everyone will get the message. Be sure to tell your teachers. This will help make it official.

Is there a less drastic way to change your name? You might keep your name but vary the spelling. Laura can become Lora or even Lori. John can convert to Jon. This way you won't be one of a dozen Johns on the class rolls. Karolyn Rose, baseball star Pete Rose's wife, opts for the *K* spelling of Carolyn. If you want to swap your ordinary name for a Muslim one, try Karim (generous) or Jamilla (beautiful).

If you're a junior or a junior miss, you may not like the confusion of carbon-copy names. The idea of being named after

Mom or Dad is fine, but there are lots of Big Bill and Little Bill mix-ups, and you may grow tired of asking, "Which Mary do you want to speak to, me or my mom?" There are ways out of this dilemma.

If you have your father's first name, take a good look at it. What variations does it offer? If you and he are both named Richard and he's Dick to all the world, you can decide to be Rick, Ricky, Rich, or Richie. Janice can keep herself separated from her mother by calling herself Jan, Jannie, or Janie. Choosing a name that is different from anyone else's in the family can avoid embarrassing moments. So declare your individuality, yet enjoy family tradition. You *can* do both.

When you are older—twenty-one, to be exact—you can change your name legally if you don't like it. (By that time, however, you may appreciate the name you always thought you couldn't stand!) You can make a name change by applying to your state or county or city court. Court action on your name isn't free. It will cost you close to $400 to trade in your name for a

new one. You'll hand out from $50 to $75 for court filing costs, $300 for a lawyer to present your case, and about $25 for the cost of typing legal documents.

For your efforts you will have a small entry in the court records and a brand-new name. The entry may look like this:

> It is on this 10th day of July 1977, adjudged that
> Mary Lys Price be and is hereby authorized to
> assume the name of Mary Lee Price, all from and
> after August 10, 1977.

Now that Mary Lee is no longer Mary Lys, she must report her new name to her bank, the Social Security office, the Bureau of Motor Vehicles of her state, the United States Government (for tax purposes), and to department stores where she has charge accounts. She must also change her voter's registration.

In 1940, Mr. Albert Przybysz of Detroit, Michigan, decided to change his name. And no wonder! It's amazing that he ever learned to spell his own last name. So what did he become? Albert Prebiz, Albert Preeb, or something even simpler? No, indeed. He changed his *first* name to Clinton. And his last name? He liked it! He was now Clinton Przybysz by law.

3 Feelings About Names

Whether you change it or not, your name never leaves you. "Good morning, Jack . . . Good night, Jack . . ." You "wear" your name all day long, and all night too. And it never wears out.

You may have strong feelings about your name or other people's names. Or perhaps other people have feelings about your name. It is strange to think that something you can't see—something that is just letters on a page or a sound in your ear—can be so important. Why is this so? Partly because sound plays an important role in names. But it is also because a name is tied to a person.

Mention a name and people will say, "Oh, that's a nice name," or, "I don't like that name." Or, "Sandy's a nice girl, but do you think her name fits her?" "Jason is my cousin's name, but he doesn't *look* like a Jason." Names and naming take up a lot of our time because we're interested in them and the persons they represent.

The strong feelings we have about names are often connected to persons we like or don't like. But sometimes it is just the name itself that draws our attention. Something about the way it sounds turns us on—or off. There is no real explanation for this. It is just that a combination of sounds hits the ear the right way or the wrong way.

And what may seem jarring to one person is quite attractive to another. People hear the same name in different ways just as the same food tastes different to different people. But it is an established fact that there are certain names that almost no one likes. These names bring to mind a boring person or a bossy person or someone who likes to pick a fight.

19

This is a serious problem, because some people have to live with these names for a lifetime. Most of us stick to our birth names and do not bother to change them legally whether we like them or not.

Do you have a neighbor your age or a pal in school with a "funny" name? A name that is too long, too hard to say, or harsh-sounding to your ear? Do you think that the person you know has a hard time living with his name?

If he does, you can help by not judging him by his name. If he's friendly and fun to be with, then he's a good guy to know. He didn't choose his name, so it shouldn't have anything to do with your friendship.

If you have just met the new girl down the block and she has a name that sounds like a soap product (Cheer, Downy, Joy), give her a chance. Or if she has a name almost as long as Mary Poppins' "supercalifragilisticexpialidocious," find a nickname that pleases you both.

When you get to like and know people with unusual names, you will soon find that the name will no longer concern you. It's the person who counts.

Names, usual or unusual, affect us in the strangest ways. Here is a case where names improve work standards. Have you ever received a package in the mail, a toy or a book perhaps, and noticed a packing slip in it? It may say something like, "Please refer to your order number if you have any questions concerning your order." The slip may also have a line reading "Carefully packaged by ———," with a name written in the blank space.

There is a story behind that blank space. Once upon a time, the space was filled in with a number: "Packaged by No. 14," for instance. The poor packer didn't even have a name! He or she was just a number. And what do you think happened? That's right—the packer often did a poor job of preparing the package for the mails.

Some mail-order companies saw that this was a mistake. They began to ask the packers to sign their own names. Packaging improved, of course. If Laura Jean or Frances packed a requested item, she wanted to be sure it was done right. After all, her name

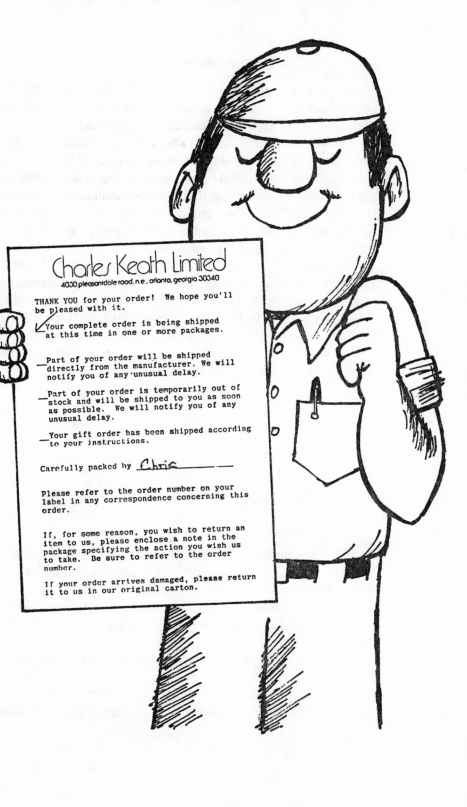

was on the mailing slip. And she was pleased to be recognized for her labor. Merchants, in adopting this new method, were once again proving that names are all-important.

In fact, our names are so important to us that we may be surprised to run into someone else with the same first name. Do you mind sharing your first name with someone else? Most people have little tricks to keep their own individuality. "Your name is Barbara too? Well, I'm Barbara *Ann,* so our names are a little bit different." "Oh, your name is John? Well, my name's Jon, spelled J-o-n, so it's really not the same."

Students at Germantown Academy, outside of Philadelphia, Pennsylvania, showed some strong opinions about names in a recent questionnaire. They are just like you, with likes and dislikes. They want to feel that their names make them special. They also appreciate the traditions surrounding their names.

Here are the names of the twenty-nine students who participated in the questionnaire:

Clare	Lisa	Gary
Elfrida	Carolyn	Erik
Ellen	Debbie	William
Donna	Ellen	Brian
Stephanie	Doug	Douglas
Elizabeth	Keith	Paul
Susan	Michael	Brad
Gretchen	Brian	John
Julia	Bob	Richard
Kimberly	John	

This might sound like the roll call in your class. If it does, it is not surprising. Parents around the country seem to favor the most recently popular names. The parents of these students seem to have pleased their offspring, because almost everyone liked his or her name. Only two students wished they could trade theirs for new ones.

Two Johns, two Brians, two Douglases, and a duet of Ellens shared names in this class of seventh-graders. And almost all the girls and boys, including the name twins, were named after a parent or a grandparent, an uncle or an aunt. One of the Douglases says that he was given his name to celebrate his Scottish heritage. "Douglas is a proud Scottish (and English) name meaning From the Black Stream."

Each student had definite ideas about what he or she would name a child someday. Names like Dominique and Meghan popped up as preferences along with *four* Jennifers. It was not surprising that Jennifer was a winning name at Germantown Academy, because it was the first choice for girls in the country just then. By the time you read this book, however, a new name may have moved to the top. Boys liked names such as Gary or Todd. Sandra got two votes from the male side as a nice name for a girl.

Why did these young people like such names as Gary and Mark, Caroline, Jill, and Jolly? One reason was that they "had a nice ring to them." "I like the way Caroline sounds," one student explained. Other names were chosen because they belonged to a brother or a sister of the student.

The names these young people chose were generally well-known names. And the students themselves have fairly common names. But these twenty-nine classmates knew friends outside their classroom with names so fascinating and unusual that they might have appeared in a "Names Around the World" dictionary. Here are some of them: Lisha, Dawn, Hugette, Alexa, Welma, Asley, Adianne, Fahim, Spenser, Frida, Eunice, Lirin, Marina, Hester, Gaudio, Ward, Damien, Mary Bell, Brooke, Merrill, Vibekye, Sax, Tanya, Bashie, Corby, Dakina.

So people have feelings about names. They like their own names. They like names that sound mysterious and exotic. And when it comes to a student questionnaire, names are way up there as a topic of interest. Everyone has a name, so everyone has an opinion!

4 *Headlined or Last-in-Line*

People like to see their names in print.

You like to see your name in print. If you make the honor roll, win a swimming trophy, or rescue a pup from a drainpipe, your name may go into the newspaper. "Jennifer Forrest Huber wins first prize in regional swim meet." You are somebody, and finally the community has recognized the fact.

Newspapers often print articles about organizations or school groups, listing the many members who form the group. Sometimes the lists go on for pages. Why do newspapers print so many names? Because they know that people like to see their names in print. And, of course, each person will buy a newspaper to look for his or her name and put it in a memory scrapbook.

Some names don't need to be in a newspaper to be noticed. They sound so important that they can surely stand up by themselves! Elliott Carter Longworth, Laura Schofield McKinstry—these must be persons going somewhere.

Why should these names sound more important than Johnny Jones or Susie Smith? It is because they have a ring and a rhythm to them—lots of important-sounding syllables all blending nicely together. The names are distinctive. They seem to be saying, "Look who I am. I'm important."

It might be nice to have an important-sounding nickname that rolls impressively off the tongue. But there are times when a simple nickname would be more welcome to its owner. When Mom or Dad or teacher is on the warpath, have you noticed how they say, "Robert House Lowther! You come here!" or, "Mary Wynne Lynch! Stop teasing your brother!" Why don't they just say, "Robbie! Come here!" or, "Mary! Stop teasing your

24

brother!" They use your full name because it gives them a l-o-n-g-e-r opportunity to catch your attention and to bawl you out. Since they almost never use your full name—three names in all, usually—you will probably stop in your tracks when you hear it.

Mostly, though, your full name has a happy ring to it. Its many letters are put together to form a name that sounds pleasant. And do you know that even the letters in that special name of yours say something about you? Letter systems have been worked out, based on beliefs that are centuries old. It is claimed that your personality can be revealed simply by the letters in your first name.

Let's take Mary, for instance. According to this theory, when a name begins with the letter *M,* the owner of this *M* name is very determined and down-to-earth and likes to travel. Robert, with the curly, curvy *R,* likes to spend money and enjoys surprising people.

So even letters are important. But did you know that some letters are more desirable than others? If your last name starts with any letter from *S* to *Z,* you are often kept waiting—for *everything.* At school, you are last on the roll call, last to go to recess. At an airport, the people in the *S* to *Z* line may board the plane after everyone else.

Some people whose last names start with the last letters of the alphabet actually suffer from being the last in line in life. This is unjust, because all names are important. One writer reports that end-of-the-alphabet people are ill more often and die at a younger age. It doesn't seem to be healthy to be kept waiting!

Some names create problems that have nothing to do with where they fall in the alphabet. How do you deal with having a famous name? What's it like to be a Paul Revere today or a John F. Kennedy or a Jimmy Carter?

Country music singer Jimmy Carter gets kidded about his name. He and President Jimmy Carter are not likely to be confused, though, because they work in very different fields. While Jimmy Carter, President, plays the political game, Jimmy Carter, singer, plays the guitar.

John Paul Jones lives outside of Philadelphia, Pennsylvania.

It seems obvious that he is a descendant of the famous naval hero. Obvious, but untrue. He is named after his father and grandfather. His occupation? Architect. Does he like the sea? Not particularly. "I'm a landlubber," he says.

Paul Revere, a resident of Boston, Massachusetts, gets phone calls in the middle of the night. People feel they must play jokes on the man whose name is synonymous with midnight rides!

Having a famous name, then, is not all the fun it might appear to be. Names like Bernice Jones or Billy Paul, pleasant but unfamiliar, may be a lot easier to live with. Of course, if another Bernice Jones or another Billy Paul enrolls in your class, then you'll have a different problem to deal with!

5 History Writes Your Name

Names are something we take for granted. After all, everyone has a name. But when you realize that your name separates you from millions of other people, you can see just how much it means.

Given names, or personal names, have always been important. Parents throughout history, whether of royal, middle-class, or peasant origin, have pondered over the best names for their babies. Even in ancient times, names counted. In the pre-Christian era an infant's name was a prize possession that was often kept secret from all but the closest members of the family. This was done partly because the baby's name was considered sacred. Such secrecy was also to prevent magicians from weaving the child's name into an evil spell which, people believed, would bring lifelong unhappiness.

Sometimes the name of a little Roman child was so secret that even the parents didn't know it. The high priest alone held this knowledge. What an extraordinary fact to learn in an age where our names are so casually tossed about! But how handy this would be for today's youngsters when they are called to wash the dishes or straighten up a room. Imagine the conversation:

> *Mom:* Please tell our son to come inside and do
> the dishes.
> *Dad:* I don't know his name.
> *Mom:* I thought you did!
> *Dad:* No, dear, don't you remember? It is such
> a secret name that *no one* knows it.

Mom: Well, just say, "Hey, you!" then.
Dad: Hey, you! . . . Gee, ten kids looked up
when I called!
Mom: Oh, well, forget it! I'll do the dishes my-
self.

Long before names were guarded secrets, people had no names at all. This was before language was invented. But as soon as people were making sounds to signify dangers and desires, they were also finding words to identify those around them.

That is exactly what the caveman did. He used a sound or word to describe an individual and to set him apart from the others. The man who ran from place to place was The Runner. Tiger was awarded to the hero who had just slain the saber-toothed tiger. A new baby delivered during the sunrise hour would be named Rosy Dawn.

Names became more descriptive as civilization advanced. Right-handed (Dexter), Gracious (Ann), and Priceless (Anthony) were more precise ways of naming people. It was natural that some names would reflect human characteristics as man grew in understanding and intelligence.

A name could also wish good luck for the newcomer. Parents blessed a brand-new squirming son with a name such as Strong (Arnold), Kind (Kevin), and Wise (Alfred). Mothers and fathers gave daughters promising names such as Loving (Pamela), Gentle (Mildred), and Pure (Katherine), and crossed their fingers.

The ancient Greeks and Romans chose names rich in meaning too. The Latin girl's name Marcia meant Of Mars. The Greek Eugene was probably of noble birth because his name meant Well-born.

Both Greek and Roman babies waited several days to be given their richly descriptive names. And when the Greek father finally decided what the infant's name would be, it was not necessarily a permanent one. Little Nicholas or Agatha might find themselves called by other names later in childhood. Father was free to change the name at any time.

Many English and American names can be traced to the

early Middle Ages as well as to ancient and Biblical times. The hearty Normans, originally fourth- and fifth-century inhabitants of the Scandinavian countries, influenced English naming after the Norman general William the Conqueror defeated England in 1066.

These ambitious, adventurous peoples from the north of France radically altered name patterns after they invaded England. Before the Normans came, the Old English, or Anglo-Saxon, names were unusual and hard to pronounce. These lusty people liked names such as Aelfheah, Swetleofu, and Burgweard.

Old English names were also different from each other. In fact, the same name was never used for more than one person. No one would have considered naming a child after a parent or a grandparent. If there was a Sigebeorht in the family, it was the only Sigebeorht.

Parents had a chance to be very creative. No traditions hampered them. They often contradicted themselves by choosing names that showed enthusiasm for warlike activities as well as respect for gentle ways.

The word "wolf" *(wulf)* often appeared as part of a child's name. Using the image of this fierce, clever animal, a parent might name a son Wulfnoth, or wolf-courage. Little Wulfnoth learned early that his parents expected great things of him.

After the Norman Conquest of 1066, the practice of making up names disappeared. William the Conqueror brought fellow soldiers with such names as Hugh and Roger, Walter and Richard, as their fathers and grandfathers were named before them.

Soon the English adopted Norman names and the custom of passing them on from father to son. But handing on a name led to some confusion. Because of the multitude of Roberts and Richards and other Norman names, it became difficult to distinguish between families. This soon led to the invention of last names, or *surnames.*

Before surnames came into common use, Thomas, the son of a hunter in one family, was kept straight from the Thomas, son of a blacksmith in another, by mentioning this relationship to their fathers. Early English records are full of examples, such as,

* CAVE WORD FORTIGER

"Thomas, son of John the Hunter, attacked Thomas, son of Walter the Blacksmith."

How would it be today if you were known as Jeffrey, son of Roger the Woodsman? Or, to be more up-to-date, how about Melanie, daughter of Stephanie the Computer Analyst, or Crosby, son of Jack the Moonwalker?

Several hundred years after Norman names had been widely accepted by the English, names from a new source were added to the many established ones. These names arose from the impact of the Catholic Church. The church was very powerful at this time and many babies were baptized with favored names such as Philip, Paul, Mary, and Elizabeth.

Girls were gifted with other names too—boys' names. Girls, if they ever wanted to be like boys, finally had their chance. But in name only! It was not at all unusual for girls to be named Nicholas, Alexander, or James.

Today, we are getting back to this custom. John Grace of Millville, New Jersey, is a mother of three and a grandmother of four. She has had no trouble with her name except for a run-in with the law. A highway patrolman, after stopping her car, glanced at her driver's license and refused to believe that her name was John.

A very tall young lady named Marshall Chapman from South Carolina finds no problem in bearing a boy's name. She is a rock 'n' roll singer who travels with the band Stars. There are Courtneys, a Cameron, and a Hilary at a private girls' school outside of Philadelphia, Pennsylvania. Michael Learned played the mother on *The Waltons* for many years. We also have many girls' names that are obviously offshoots of masculine names. Michelle is the feminine of Michael; Roberta, of Robert.

So far, there is no reverse trend. Parents are not naming boys Patricia or Katherine. Maybe they realize that their sons would have a tough time of it as did Sue in singer Johnny Cash's song, "A Boy Named Sue."

However, there are a few names shared by boys and girls. President Harry Truman's brother, Vivian, was a farmer. Close friends of composer Jules Stein called him Julie. And two of football's big bad boys—Lynn Swann, Pittsburgh Steeler wide receiver, and June Jones, 200-pounder with the Atlanta Falcons —bear names that are distinctly feminine.

Lynne Carter, well-known night club actor, chooses to spell his name differently from that of the sports hero, Lynn Swann. Chris, of course, is a nickname shared by Christophers and Christians as well as Christines and Christinas. Lindsay, Laurie, Stacey, and Hilary are shared by both sexes. Only one example comes to mind from history where a man was provided with a woman's name. Lord Anne Hamilton (1709–1748) was named after his godmother, Queen Anne.

England had many religious upheavals from its late medieval period through the reign of Elizabeth I. When Oliver Cromwell and the Puritans seized power in 1649, they forced English citizens to put aside their worldly ways and lead more godly and serious lives. To make their point, the Puritans gave their children names that would discourage them from being too gay or happy-go-lucky. Names like Live-Again, Praise-God, and Earthly Dust were to remind a child of his purpose on earth. One father even named his child Read-the-Bible-Every-Night. Many other youngsters were given four- and five-word names with a thought to live up to. It is good that such traditions have not extended into the twentieth century, or parents might decide to name a child Do-Your-Homework-Every-Night Smith! One father, not too long ago, did build an issue into his son's name. Hardy Lawrence, president of Braniff Airlines, named his son States Rights, to represent his father's political opinions.

The end of Puritan rule halted the custom of giving these forbidding names. People went back to happy names for their children. Girls had pretty names based on flowers, such as Daisy, Fern, Holly, Lily, and Rose. This custom has extended into the twentieth century with Lady Zinnia Pollock, of Chipping Camden, England, enlarging the circle of flower names.

Although the seventeenth century eased away from the heavy-handed names of the previous century, some youngsters still had names that would make pretty tough going for children today. Ferdinand, Marmaduke, Griselda, and Theodosia are not exactly names you would like to take to school with you.

But there were plenty of common names at that time too—names like Andrew and Amy—that we are comfortable with today. And almost all of these "comfortable" names are fine old names from previous centuries and different places.

The traditions and hopes of centuries of world citizens have filtered down to us through names. The story of names is the story of civilization. Reading about them is an enjoyable way of learning about our past.

6 *Last Names Then and Now*

Double-decker surnames with the last name on top began to make their appearance in ninth-century France. Does John Doe as printed below look strange to you?

Doe
John

The French adopted surnames long before the British. It was not until the 1200's that surnames caught on in England. But even as it grew increasingly popular to add a last name to a first one, not everyone did so. Farmer Richard Goodwin's neighbor next door may have stubbornly remained simply the farmer, Arthur.

But, in time, the English adopted many last names to cut down on the confusion created by identical first names. In 1465, Edward IV helped to stabilize the situation by requiring all English subjects to adopt surnames. His law stated: "They shall take unto them a surname, either of some Towne or some Colour as Blacke or Brown, or some Arte or Science as Smyth or Carpenter, or some office as Cooke or Butler."

King Edward was only making official what people had been doing for centuries. A great many names had developed from the give-and-take of everyday living. The sea, the land, the marketplace, the home, daily work, all contributed to the naming process.

Last names must have been a relief to citizens tired of the confusion of so many similar first names. It is fun to think of how some of Edward's subjects may have decided upon their new last names. It is easy to imagine how William's son Roger became Roger Williamson, and his son John, John Williamson.

Naturally, most name changes were not planned. They just happened. Except for those encouraged by the king, the additions just appeared as time passed. Man, as usual, was trying to cut down on the confusion in his life. Adding surnames was one way to do it.

Once last names were established, they were usually handed on from generation to generation. But some historians believe that a surname was not always inherited from the father. Either the son chose his own or it was given to him by the people in his community. William Camden, a sixteenth-century historian, mentions a man with eight sons, each with a different last name. How strange such a situation would seem to us today! If John and Mary Armistead down the street sent out a Christmas card with greetings from them and their eight boys, it might read something like this:

Merry Christmas
from
John and Mary Armistead
Phil Price
Ralph Wilson
Jim Leslie
Jeff Tate
Bob Forrest
Rick Lee
Bill Batch
Colin Stephens

Today, everyone in the United States has a last name. It is almost always the same name as the parent family. It is one of twenty thousand American surnames inherited from at least forty different countries. But of these twenty thousand names, just thirty are shared by twenty million of us! Among the most prevalent last names are Smith, Johnson, Williams, Jones, and Brown. There are actually twenty-seven columns of Smiths in the New York City telephone directory. And the variations on Smith— Smithson, Smithers, Smythe, and many others—add up to many millions of people bearing this surname.

Allen, another popular last as well as first name representing thousands of families today, reaches back to claim kinship with a first name, Aethelwine. Aethelwine was one of those Old English names before the Norman Conquest that needed no last name. Many others are obviously descendants of the sturdy, highly individual first names used before the eleventh century.

An author, Constance Mary Matthews, was able to make the connection between these very old names and the presently used ones by checking every source of names from the *Domesday Book* of 1086 to today's London telephone directory. The place to study names, Mrs. Matthews realized, is where names are recorded. The *Domesday Book* provides endless lists of names, thanks to the decision of William I (William the Conqueror) to take a census for tax purposes. Historians have scoured every source, from ancient records of baptism to the seventeenth century's greengrocers' customer lists, to discover history's names.

Everyone has played Twenty Questions. The first question in determining the name of the mystery item asks, Is it animal, vegetable, or mineral? Names don't count in this game because without their "owners" they are not real. But people names can also be animal, vegetable, or mineral. Beaver, Pepper, Rock, Tree, and Brook are examples of names that have come from nature.

Relationship was another factor in naming. Besides the attachment of "son" to a name to show belonging, the father-son relationship was also indicated by certain prefixes. Fitz-, Mac-, O'-, Up-, and Ap- are variations of "son of."

Place-names too were popular as surnames. The young man who left his hometown to move far away could take it with him by adopting the town name as his surname. James of the beautiful cathedral town of Wells became James Wells. His neighbor, Gerald, living near a small enclosed area bounded by rolling hills, might be identified as Gerald Worth. "Worth" is the Anglo-Saxon word for enclosure. Tyrone and Sylvester represent land and woods. They are used as first or last names.

Remember the way some persons' first names developed because of a distinct feature or mannerism? This is the way *last* names were often chosen too. If *your* last name is Black or White, or Large or Little, one of your ancestors was probably dark or fair, big or small.

Surely the most easily traced last names are those dealing with occupations. Today's Bakers, Carters, Cooks, and Coopers had ancestors who were engaged in baking or cooking, or in such work as hauling (Carter) or barrelmaking (Cooper). Generally the name of an occupation was chosen after the family had been in the same line of work for several generations. The potter who taught his son the art of pottery-making was gratified to see his grandson take up the potter's wheel, too. By the time the great-grandson had been apprenticed to the trade, it was natural that he would take Potter as a last name.

Many Americans have last names that reflect foreign languages. But in many of the original homelands of today's Americans, last names were chosen in the same way as those of the English. In Germany, for instance, familiar surnames are often as descriptive as in England. Weiss means White; Klein, Small. Names ending in -bach (brook), -horst (wood), and -burg (castle) show that the Germans also identified themselves by choosing landmarks as a part of their names.

Many Italian surnames came about through nicknames. The young man who flitted about like a firefly was called Lucciola. The curly-headed fellow was Rizzo. Other Italian names are compound names—two names put together. These are descriptive terms just like Mr. Long and Mr. Short. Bonadonna is Good Woman and Belviso means Pretty Face.

In medieval German cities, the Jews were often named after the drawing on a sign posted at their home. Herr Loeb took his name from the lion on his sign; Strauss had a bouquet-picture to thank for his name. Two houses in Frankfurt were identified with the sign of the eagle. House number 27 had a black eagle, and house number 86 a golden eagle. Eagle in German is Adler. Numerous Adlers in America verify the popularity of this name.

The Jewish people, too, chose names after their occupations. The name Arzt means Doctor; Sofer, Letter Writer. Polish and Russian Jews owe many of their names to geography, occupations and appearance too. Alkus or Algus is a name that developed from the Yiddish for Olkusz, a town in Poland. Altfield is Yiddish for Staropol, meaning Old Field in Polish. And Szupak? It means Sandpaper in Polish. The name explains itself when you realize that sandpaper is used in cabinetmaking. The first Szupaks were obviously craftsmen.

Many surnames do not seem to have any meaning. Their history is often hidden in Old English words and phrases or in the native language of America's earliest immigrants. Many unrecognizable names are descriptions of people and places and happenings. There are often conflicting opinions about the real meaning behind such names. Take Esposito, for instance. Some say the name reflects the tale of an abandoned baby left on the doorstep of an Italian church several hundred years ago. Another interpretation is that it simply involves two persons joined together in marriage.

Women throughout history have followed their own way of leaving the past behind. They have abandoned their names at the church door upon marriage. Interestingly enough, men too sometimes gave up their names when they took their marriage vows. If there was wealth and land on the woman's side, a man might sacrifice his name to perpetuate his wife's more prominent one.

This unusual custom is rarely in practice today. A possible scenario:

> *Barbara Richlady:* Alfred, will you promise to love, honor, and respect me *and* take my name?
>
> *Alfred Poorman:* Are you kidding? If you want to marry me, you'll have to be willing to be Mrs. Poorman and have a lot of little baby Poormans for me.
>
> *Barbara Richlady:* But, darling, in my family inheritance, it says I lose all my money and estates if I give up my name!
>
> *Alfred Poorman:* Gee, that's tough! We wouldn't want all those ancestors of yours to get upset. All right. I'll make the supreme sac-

rifice and become Mr. Richlady. But I want a
little Richman along with all the little Richladys
you're going to give me.

Dropping and adding names was not just a consideration of
marriage. Throughout the early history of British surnames, men
often dropped and picked up surnames on a whim. If a tradesman
or farmer didn't like his old name, he adopted a new one without
so much as a nod to the local registry.

Today, we are still free to change our names if we have a
convincing reason. But we must do so within the limits of the law.
Surnames are no longer left to caprice. A Carter must remain a
Carter whether he carts goods or not; a Smith is still a Smith
whether or not he or she shoes horses. Mr. Good, Ms. Rich, and
Mrs. Fine must remain as they are named, too. But with names
like those, why trade?

7 *A Coat of Arms for Your Name*

Many families consider their last name one of their most valuable possessions. Prominent family names stand for wealth and tradition. Sometimes a family crest, or coat of arms, illustrates family status in a graphic, refined way.

In the past, coats of arms belonged strictly to the titled and wealthy of the British Isles and Europe. Their original purpose was not to impress, but to protect! When manor lords or knights at court fought bloody battles for land, ladies, and Christianity, they were shielded by heavy armor. They were so thoroughly encased in these costumes of war that they sometimes couldn't tell who were allies and who were enemies.

Royal fighters soon solved this problem by embroidering designs on their banners. But often a duke designed an insigne for his crest only to find himself challenging an enemy lord bearing much the same design. The Heralds' College was established in England in 1483 to award crests, ease confusion, and avoid duplication. Later, when it was no longer necessary to use the crests as identification, they remained as badges of honor.

The Heralds' College, now known as the College of Arms, still has the final word on who may claim "bearings." A family's claim must clearly show a connection with the original family bearing the heraldic design. This connection must be made through the male side. A woman cannot claim a coat of arms, but she is permitted to use her family's design in a piece of jewelry, on a scarf, or on stationery.

Today's College of Arms is headed by the Duke of Norfolk and his retinue of kings of arms. They handle family claims to historic coats of arms, and also award new ones to deserving

private individuals, towns, and businesses.

One request that came up not too long ago involved none other than the future husband of England's only princess. In 1973, Princess Anne became engaged to Captain (then Lieutenant) Mark Phillips of the Queen's Dragoon Guards. The young equestrian and soldier claimed no existing coat of arms, so one had to be designed.

And it had to be designed in a hurry! The wedding cakes for the most important royal wedding of the decade needed the traditional arms, crest, and motto to set them off in all their elegance.

The College of Arms happily accepted the challenge of creating a new coat of arms. A meeting was arranged to come up with a heraldic emblem both magnificent and appropriate to the young man's interests.

The formal description of Captain Phillips' coat of arms sounds as though the words are shaken up like dice and thrown out randomly. They don't make much sense to us (the College uses a special vocabulary), but they roll off the tongue gloriously:

> ARMS: Per chevron Azure and Or in chief, a horse courant Argent and in base a sprig of forget-me-not flowered, slipped and leaved proper
>
> CREST: On a wreath of the colours a spur rowel upward or, winged argent enclosing a lozenge Sable
>
> MOTTO: PRO REGE ET PATRIA (for King and Country)

In short, Mark Phillips' coat of arms reflects his interest in horses, in his regiment, and in his country. The lozenge Sable, or black diamond (just below the rowel, or small wheel with sharp points at the end of the spur), symbolizes coal mining, his ancestors' occupation. The motto "For King and Country" seems just right for a young man marrying into the royal family.

Captain Phillips had some unexpected flourishes added to

PRO REGE·ET PATRIA

his emblem a year after he was awarded the coat of arms. Princess Anne's car with the princess and her new husband inside was held up, and Captain Phillips' swift actions helped bring the dangerous encounter to a quick end. The captain was made a Commander of the Royal Victorian Order for his bravery, and a ribbon and badge were added to his coat of arms.

Heraldry is a complex art with strict rules. Only certain colors are permitted and each part of the design has a special meaning. The shield in a coat of arms has a field divided invisibly into four areas. These areas are described in the language of heraldry. For instance, if there is a lion in the lower right section of the shield, you say that it is in the "dexter base." People not versed in the art would say that the three bold stars in President George Washington's coat of arms covered the *top* of his shield. But heraldry would position the stars in the "dexter chief," "middle chief," and "sinister chief" portions of the shield.

Washington's coat of arms dates back to fifteenth-century England. Examples of it crop up in succeeding generations of Washingtons. The crest is carved on the gravestone of Sir John Washington, late-seventeenth-century English ancestor of our first President. The Washington family (those with direct claim to this particular branch of the family) still uses the crest today. Since George Washington had no children, there is no direct descendant using the coat of arms, but relatives directly related to the family display it with pride.

Why do people reach into their pasts to discover whether they have a coat of arms? They do so because this distinguished seal identifies them as members of an established family or clan. It gives them a feeling of belonging in a world that is fast-moving and impersonal.

If you are interested in finding out whether you have a coat of arms in your family, visit the genealogy section of your city library or the city historical society. If you do not live near such sources, you can send a letter of inquiry. You can also write to your state library and check with county and township historical societies.

But remember when checking into your name to be sure that it is connected to a family bearing the heraldic design. For instance, some Smith, Jones, and Nicholson families have coats of arms, but not everyone bearing these names can claim a connection.

On with the search! But if you find you can't connect with any of the arms-bearing families, you can design a coat of arms for yourself or your school club. Sketch in your interests and occupations. It won't get the stamp of approval from the College of Arms, but it will be original—and all yours!

8 *First Names Around the World*

What are some of the different customs in naming a baby around the world? Mothers and fathers worldwide have so many traditions to follow, so many names they can choose from. But to each parent, whatever the tradition, the name given to his or her child makes it the most important baby in the world.

In Japan, children are often numbered instead of named. Ichiko means number one child, or firstborn. Brother number two would be Nichiko. At the age of fifteen, a young boy may take on another name that reflects the social standing of the family or the father's business. A Japanese boy's name, then, may also be a kind of title.

The Nigerian baby is loved and watched over by the entire community. Relatives and neighbors as well as parents welcome the baby into their close-knit society.

The Nigerian (Yoruban) naming ceremony is very special and very beautiful. The family history of the new infant is set forth before the happy crowd gathered for the occasion. And even the spirits of ancestors are welcomed to join the ceremony and bless the child.

The baby is then treated to little tastes of honey, wine, water, salt, and pepper. A bit of each is dropped on the tiny tongue. These represent all the elements needed for a happy life. The honey guarantees happiness; the wine, good wishes; and the water is sustainer of life itself. The salt gives life its flavor, and the pepper its spice. If the baby does not sneeze after a sample of the pepper, he or she is off to a good start!

Francis Selormey, now director of the Central Organization of Sports in Ghana, remembers the birth of his little sister and her

47

introduction to society. He recalls a very colorful aspect of the time-honored Yoruban naming ceremony: "One of the women in the group rushed forward and picked up the baby saying, 'Whose precious child is this? I have found it. Who will pay me for this child?' My mother then stepped out of her room for the first time and said, 'I will.' She paid a token price of a penny and received her child back." The payment was symbolic—it simply reaffirmed the great value of the child.

The names selected for Nigerian babies have lovely sounds and inspirational meanings. Parents who name their son Oladele (pronounced aw-lah-day-lay) hope that he will bring "honors and wealth" to the home. In naming a baby Folayan, parents know that she will "walk in dignity" all her life.

A child's name is on trial in some African tribes. If the newly named baby frets and cries for several months, it is a sign that the name is not suitable for the child. He is then given another and everyone hopes that he will coo and gurgle to show his approval.

In France it doesn't pay to be original about names. French citizens must choose from a list of selected names for their new baby, or the child will not be recognized by French law. When Jean-Jacques Le Goarnic gave his six children unofficial names, they were denied their citizenship. Adraboaren, Maiwenn, Gwendal, Diwezha, Sklerjenn, and Brann, ages twelve to nineteen, have only recently been recognized by the French government and accepted as citizens. Their father took his case to the World Court and, after a twenty-year struggle, the youngsters are now legal citizens. If Monsieur Le Goarnic had failed in his effort, the six young Le Goarnics would never have been allowed to drive a car in France, marry in their native country, or enlist in the French army.

French law still states that parents must choose names from the official register, but now there are a greater number of acceptable first names. With the approval of foreign names, some nicknames, and different spellings, French parents will soon have almost as much choice as citizens of other countries.

But then there are problems with last names. The Trognons, a French couple, were denied adoption rights unless they were willing to change their last name. Trognon means Core (of a pear or apple) or Stump (of a cabbage) and the judge in the adoption case objected to a name with such meanings. He was afraid that the adopted children would be ridiculed.

American Indian names are melodious and original. When translated, they delight the ear and please the eye. White Shell, Flower-of-the-World, and Looking-Glass Yellow are among the beautiful word names chosen to fit a winsome new baby.

There are many different naming customs among American Indian tribes. These customs enrich the name of an Indian baby with their mystical meanings. For instance, a child may receive an animal name if Father is out hunting during the baby's birth. When Father returns, the child is given the name of the animal killed during the hunt.

Sometimes an Indian child is named after an event in a dream. Other children have two names, one for winter and one for summer. Some names may be loaned out as the child grows up, while others may be given away if their owners are in the market for another. The young Indian who is quite happy with his birth name may suddenly decide to exchange it for a military title. A pretty Indian lass who answers to Rain-in-the-Face may change her name to fit her new occupation—in translation, Dry Goods Woman.

Some American Indians collect names as others would collect charms for a bracelet. It is not unusual for an Indian child to have nine or ten names, each bestowed upon him or her to mark important occasions.

Many American Indians have names of the English-speaking world. A William or a Katherine is not unusual for an Indian babe. But tribes like the Yakima Indians of the State of Washington retain the right to bestow traditional Indian names through the time-honored ceremonies of formal name-giving.

Brazilians feel that first names are more important than last names. In fact, the Brazilian citizen is sometimes listed in telephone books, civic organizations, and other formal lists by his or her Christian name. Parents often give a child a name that begins with *A* so that the youngster will head the list.

This first-name system would come in handy in our country. Because our last names are inherited, we have no choice about where they fall in the alphabet. So anyone whose name is among the *S*'s to *Z*'s is doomed to bring up the rear every time. But in Brazil, because parents can choose a first name, they can guarantee their child a place near the top. The only problem is that there may be three hundred Anas or Antonios in a telephone book or on a newspaper subscription list.

In Hawaii, boys and girls receive names as rich in meaning as those of the American Indians. But with traditional Hawaiian names there is a difference. Names like My Jewel or Brave One may be used for either a boy or a girl. With the new insistence on equality for women, the old-fashioned Hawaiian names are very useful.

We put titles such as Mr., Ms., Mrs., or Miss at the beginning of names. The Vietnamese do it another way. The middle names of these Oriental people often indicate a boy or a girl, so there is no need for introductory titles. Vietnamese last names, incidentally, are often very short. La, Ta, and Do sound like notes in a musical scale. One thing is certain—they are easy to spell. An American kindergartner learning to spell her name would be delighted to have a two-letter surname. If her last name was Higgenbottom or Raffensperger, she would surely like to trade names with a Vietnamese lass whose last name was Si.

There are many other customs around the world. Here are some of them:

In Purim Kukis in the Minipur State of China, a tightly knit band of residents make their own name rules. If any member of one tribe takes the name of a member of a neighboring tribe, he must hand over a pig and a pot of rice. But once he has handed over these gifts, he is allowed to keep his stolen name.

Many Swedes owe their colorful, warlike names to their Norse ancestors. Their names are full of challenge and bravado —hardly typical of today's peaceful Swedes.

In China, the surnames are written first, the first name last. In America, the names would appear as Anderson John and Jones Lenore.

In Korea, last names come first—sometimes with tragic consequences. Not many years ago, two young Koreans studying in New York met, fell in love, and *then* exchanged names. A name is such a personal thing to the Koreans and many other Orientals that it is not shared until the owner feels comfortable about divulging it.

The two young people, upon learning that they both had the name Kim, were forced to give each other up and seek other mates. Because they each had the identical last name, it was obvious that they had a common male ancestor. It is against Korean law to marry someone to whom you are related on the male side.

In this case, Kim Su Ro, born in A.D. 41, was the common male ancestor of these two unlucky lovers. Legend says that Kim Su Ro was conceived from a golden egg. Golden eggs are often thought of as good-luck symbols. But to a hundred thousand present-day Kims unfortunate enough to fall in love with a fellow Kim, the golden egg is no prize.

In some countries, two is a magic number. That is, twins are considered to be supernatural—not quite like other infants. The Nuer, an African tribe, feel that birds and twins are both very unusual. They honor the rare newborn look-alikes by reserving beautiful bird names for them.

There are many interesting naming customs among the Jews. These are customs that know no homeland, because many Jews all over the world follow them. One tradition follows the rule that the aunt or uncle, grandmother or grandfather has prior owner-ship to a name. This means that a parent had better find a brand-new one for a newborn.

Some Jews "fence" with the Angel of Death when a new baby is very ill. They feel that there really is such a bad angel, and they try to confuse him. If the wicked Messenger is looking for a little boy named David who is deathly ill, the parents might change the boy's name to Samuel. The Angel of Death will pass by the sick "Samuel," because he is looking for David to take with him.

Despite the many names and naming customs around the

world, there are some things that never change. Parents every-where take time to name their babies because they love them. And they tend to choose names that have always been popular in their own countries.

Actually, there are several names that are popular in many, many countries. Sometimes these names sound like each other —sometimes they don't. Let's look at Barbara and Richard in countries many travel-hours away from each other.

ENGLISH	Barbara	Richard
CZECH	Barbara	Richard
FRENCH	Barbe	Richard
GERMAN	Barbara	Richard
GREEK	Voska	Rihardos
HUNGARIAN	Barbola	Ricard
ITALIAN	Barbara	Riccardo
LATVIAN	Barbar	Risardas
POLISH	Barbara	Ryszard
PORTUGUESE	Barbara	Ricardo
RUMANIAN	Varvara	Dic
RUSSIAN	Varvara	Rostislav
SERBO-CROATIAN	Varvara	Rihard
SPANISH	Bárbara	Ricardo
SWEDISH	Barbro	Rickard
UKRANIAN	Varvaru	Rostyslav

That's a lot of Barbaras and Richards, or Varvaras and Ricar-dos!

9 *First Names for U.S. Children*

Three million or more babies are born in the United States each year. This means that six million or more persons are talking about whether the newborn is going to bear great-grandmother's name or be named after a relative, a movie hero or heroine, or even the current President. No wonder the subject of names is so popular!

Most parents will choose a North American name. But did you know that, except for the American Indian names, there is no truly North American name? There are United States customs and trends in naming, but we have to look elsewhere for the origin of the names themselves.

To this day, names most popular in fifteenth-century England remain in the running. William, John, and Thomas, Elizabeth, Mary, and Ann keep popping up as the centuries pass. Small Williams and Marys visited country fairs in the 1600's. Small Williams and Marys today get their entertainment via television. Times change; many names do not.

Such familiar names as John, William, Victoria, and Elizabeth became popular because children were named after the reigning monarchs of the time. A rash of Elizabeths named after England's present queen shows that this still happens. One person can influence many people in the very personal area of name-giving.

The popular names William and Richard reach back to the days of the great hero. The adventures of William the Conqueror and Richard the Lion-Hearted prompted peasants and landowners to name their children after these bold warriors.

Today's names for girls that have lasted through the centuries were not often inspired by heroines and royalty. There were few role models for women in the early days of history. But favorite names had their own traditions. Feminine names were lovingly passed on from mother to daughter, carefully chosen to flatter a grandmother. The saints were popular sources for girls' names, too. Elizabeth, Margaret, Ann, and Mary led the roll call in sixteenth-century England. Four hundred years later, these names are still among the most popular.

Except for John and Elizabeth, the top names for boys and girls do not include the old favorites, but they do not rank too far behind. Most recently, Michael, David, Joseph, John, Jason, Christopher, Anthony, Robert, James, and Daniel have been chosen over all other names. Winners of the name-popularity contest for girls are Jennifer, Jessica, Nicole, Melissa, Michele, Elizabeth, Danielle, Maria, and Christine.

Whether your name is Jennifer or Ginny, Bob or Ted, you have a choice in the way you sign your name. Americans have seven different forms for their signatures. Let's say your first name is Elizabeth, your middle name is Murray, and your surname is Brown. You are used to being Betsy Brown, but you may also be:

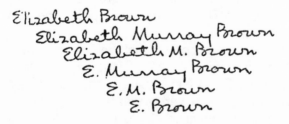

The way you sign your name tells a lot about you as a person. If it is E. Brown, you like to get things done in a hurry. If it is Elizabeth Murray Brown, you are a very formal person. If you like E. Murray Brown, you are out to impress others—and maybe yourself too.

If your name is Jennifer, you share the name that topped recent popularity lists. Julie Nixon Eisenhower, daughter of President Nixon, named her baby Jennie. The elegant Guinevere and the short, informal Jen or Jenny are from the same name family as Jennifer. All the variations are Welsh and mean Fair Lady.

Jennifer is a name you will find anywhere in the United States of America. It is not a regional name. Neither is Ginny or Ted. These are names that can be found in any of the fifty states.

But a few names do characterize a particular group or geographical section. For example, the names Hannah and Eliza belong to the colonial Quaker tradition. Southern names such as Beauregard and Jerry Lee are regional. Double names such as Jerry Lee or Becky Lou are Dixie favorites. Rosalynn (pronounced ROZ-a-lan) Carter, President Carter's wife, has a distinctly Southern name. It is doubly pretty when pronounced with a Southern accent.

Hollywood names have their own character, too. They are names dreamed up for stars, names that light up in the mind as well as on the marquee. Find a name to fit an image and you may be on the way to success. Rip Torn and Julie Andrews are catchy, perky names that send the public to the movie screen.

Spangler Arlington Brugh changed his name to Robert Taylor and Doris von Kappelhoff to Doris Day, to smooth the road to stardom. But real-name stars are more the style today. Sylvester Stallone and John Travolta, Candice Bergen and Talia Shire are good examples.

Some stars are so popular that their names surface in nurseries all over the United States. If Jane Doe of Hoboken, New Jersey, can't be Olivia Newton-John, she can at least name her child after the lovely singer. If you have ever seen Clark Gable movies, you will understand the great star's popularity. And when he played Rhett Butler in *Gone with the Wind,* in 1939, there were several little Rhetts registered on state birth records soon after.

More recently, Kunta and Kizzy became popular names for black children after the television adaptation of Alex Haley's *Roots.*

Hollywood stars often changed their names to simplify them or make them sound less ethnic. But there is a trend now among some Americans to discard their fairly commonplace names and

return to the exotic, melodious names of their ancestors.

Many black Americans are choosing the ethnic names of their forebears and glorying in their newly discovered heritage. Some of these names are still popular in present-day Africa. LeRoi Jones, the playwright, chose the name Imamu Baraka. Champion prizefighter Cassius Clay, for example, reappeared with the spiritual title of Muhammad Ali.

Other blacks choose African names to give their lives dignity and meaning. Some, like Clay, opt for the Arabic names of Northern African countries that practice the religion of Islam. These people call themselves Muslims and follow the teachings of the prophet Muhammad. Jones-now-Baraka also had chosen an Arabic name, but quite possibly it is also East African or Swahili.

Many blacks today search for unusual names that will focus attention on their children. Black parents think long and hard about the names their children will bear. Choices like Tiwauni and Kareem show an ear for colorful, musical names.

But black names are usually indistinguishable from names of other groups. The most popular names in a recent survey of black college students were: Deborah, Sandra, Patricia, Beverly, Cynthia, Barbara, Mary, Denise, Jacqueline, Catherine, Betty, Janice, Carolyn, Linda, Marsha, Gail, Joyce, Brenda, Gwendolyn, Constance, Karen, Marilyn.

Young black men's names were: Michael, Robert, Charles, William, Edward, John, Richard, Ronald, Gregory, Kenneth, Francis, Paul, Raymond, Samuel, Donald, Joseph, Victor, Ernest, Thomas.

A list of white students for that year was not very different. This shows that certain names have appeal no matter what ethnic group is involved.

While many popular ethnic names are longer and more traditional, another trend is toward shortening formal names. Names like Liza and Meg are considered quite acceptable. And in this case, Liza doesn't stand for Elizabeth, nor is Meg short for Margaret. Liza and Meg may well be the formal names registered on the birth certificate. Jack and Ray are examples of boys' names that stand quite solidly on their own.

Twins and triplets may be given shortened names, long names, rhyming names, names starting with the same letter. But often, multiple names like Annie and Aggie, or Tim, Jim, and Kim tend to make twins and triplets carbon copies rather than individuals. And wearing a look-alike outfit, a same-name twin can't be sure he has an identity of his own.

Lately, the trend among mothers and dads of double or triple blessings is to give them names that do not sound alike. These parents are also asking that their children be placed in different grade sections in school. This gives look-alikes a chance to develop their own personalities. It also keeps them from standing in for each other and turning the classroom into a guessing game!

Christmas of 1978 had a special gift (or gifts) for Grace Ho of New York—three little Hos. Laurine, Lisa, and Linda, with names admittedly alike, were dandy holiday presents. Someday these triplets will fill Santa's lap as they whisper birthday-Christmas wishes into his ear.

10 *Middle Names and Last Names First*

Middle names may be squeezed in between first names and last names, but they serve a very important purpose. A middle name gives parents a chance to bring family history into their offspring's name. Choices such as Mother's maiden name or the name of a prominent ancestor give a name meaning.

John Mirkil Carter gets a grandmother's maiden name, Mirkil, into the picture. In bearing the middle name Ambler, Harold Ambler Wilcox establishes a link with his relatives, the Ambler family, and the Pennsylvania town of Ambler, named after a heroic lady ancestor.

Middle names can also keep different generations of the same family from getting mixed up with one another. Gordon Connolly Jackson names his son Gordon Wood Jackson. This cuts down the confusion between the names of father and son, while still allowing Dad to name a son after him. The choice of a different middle name for a son is a good way to avoid the confusion that "junior" can create.

First names are often used as middle names. Both John Kyle Carter and Nancy Sheila Wadsworth are able to choose either given name as the one they want to use.

Once upon a time there were no middle names. Even in the eighteenth century it was Geoffrey Hunter or Priscilla Longworth. The use of middle names as a custom did not appear until the early nineteenth century. Only three signers of the Declaration of Independence had middle names. George Washington and Thomas Jefferson had first and last names only, a fact that didn't seem to hold back either of them.

Not everyone has a middle name today. Parents unable to

agree on one sometimes decide not to include it. This may make such a name appear a bit brief, but that is no great catastrophe. And should a no-middle-name individual join the Navy, that person receives a nice new middle initial. James Irwin becomes James "n" Irwin. The "n" stands for no middle name.

Robert Price, an electrical engineer who lives in Massachusetts, has no middle name. And unlike Harry S Truman (the S doesn't stand for anything, so it's written without a period), he doesn't even have a middle initial. Mr. Price says that sometimes credit card companies will insert a middle initial even though he has none. The fact is that some computers handling name-processing simply cannot "accept" a name without a middle initial. Mr. Price, as a scientist familiar with computers, has bowed to the bossy machine's omnipotence. Now and then he thinks about adding an initial. He has fiddled around with such ideas as S for Space, or $\emptyset$, a mathematical symbol. But it looks as though he will remain Robert Price—a name distinguished by its lack of pretension.

Mr. Price's sons, on the other hand, are rich in middle names. Stephen Price's middle name is Livingstone. His great-great-great-uncle was the famous explorer Dr. David Livingstone. Colin Llewellyn Price is named after his two grandfathers. His full name reflects some favorite name choices of the British Isles. Colin is English, Llewellyn and Price are Welsh. And when the parents, Robert and Jennifer Price, chose Hazleton as a middle name for their youngest son, Teddy, they were honoring two prominent relatives on the Price side.

In contrast to Robert Price and his compact name, there is one young man who has several middle names. He is England's Prince Charles, also known as Charles Philip Arthur George, Prince of Wales.

Royalty places great importance on a name—or names. The names of a new baby prince or princess are chosen to reflect the child's royal history. Some of the names may include those of the parents and grandparents and an illustrious ancestor who has trotted through history, winning empires.

Royalty seldom uses last names, although some members do

have them. Last names are for the less famous and the less wealthy—that is, all the rest of us.

Some middle names, like last names, have a swashbuckling history. Evelyn deZouch Anderson, a Maine resident, traces her name back to the England of moated castles, local skirmishes, kingly favors, and impressive titles.

The castle manor of Ashby near Birmingham, England, was granted to Hugh de Grantmeisnil by William I in the eleventh century. It was passed on by marriage to the Zouch family (the *de* of the present deZouch was added later) and remained in their possession for many years. The castle is now a ruin, but the name deZouch is very much intact.

DeZouch, then, was once a last name. Now it is a middle name. Some last names even become first names. As early as the eighteenth century, parents were electing a last name as a first name for the baby. Sara and John Winthrop might choose Sara's maiden name, Rogers, for their new baby boy. You can bet that Rogers Winthrop would be very special to his mother.

Today, names like Wharton Sinkler, Reed Rafetto, and Hendren (a girl) Thornton ring impressively in the ear. Although youngsters bearing last-names-first may have a little explaining to do, they generally like their unusual names.

Last names as first names can be very formal. You can go to extremes in other directions too. What is the most informal first name? An initial-name, of course, or more commonly, two initials. This has been a very popular custom in the southern United States, for example, B. J. Jones or T. R. Thomas. In other cases B. J. may stand for Betty Jane and T. R. for Thomas Rex. It is unlikely that the parents gave these youngsters initial-nicknames. Probably they were dubbed with the initials by friends, and like it or not, they will continue with those nicknames throughout life.

11 *Social Groups Force Name Changes*

Using initials is one of many ways to adapt or change your name. But no change of name is so dramatic as the direction that naming is taking as a result of the women's liberation movement.

Actually, women's names are not changing—at least not when it comes to marriage. Many young women are deciding to keep their family names when they marry. Or a young woman may combine her name with her husband's and put a hyphen between the two, for example, Mrs. Lee-Forrest. By keeping her family name, a young woman is, in a sense, keeping her own identity. She is a wife, but is her own person, too. Other women feel that they can assume their husband's name and still keep their own identity.

Let's eavesdrop on a conversation between newly engaged Stephanie Swartz and her friend Wynne. It illustrates the choices a young woman has today when she marries.

> *Wynne:* Oh, Stephanie, you're so lucky to be getting married. When is the big day?
> *Stephanie:* July twenty-second. Then (she says proudly) I'll be Mrs. Daniel Forrest, or—
> *Wynne:* Or Stephanie Swartz-Forrest.
> *Stephanie:* Right. Or even Stephanie Swartz.
> *Wynne:* Well, which do you think it will be?
> *Stephanie:* Well, if I'm Mrs. Daniel Forrest, Stephanie Swartz has disappeared completely from the scene. I'm not sure I like that. If I remain Stephanie Swartz, I won't have the pleasure of sharing my husband's name. But if I'm Stephanie Swartz-Forrest, I'll have the best of every-

thing. I'll have to think about it.

Wynne: Well, Stephanie Swartz, Stephanie Swartz-Forrest, or Stephanie Forrest, whoever you are, be sure that I catch the bridal bouquet!

Women as marriage partners have come a long way from the days of seventeenth- and eighteenth-century England when they were considered chattel. Chattel means property, and that is exactly what a married woman was—property of the male. But this bondage wasn't totally undesirable, because times were severe and a woman needed the physical and financial protection of a man. By assuming his name, she was his property and his responsibility as well.

But today, when such laws and traditions are outmoded and unnecessary, only two states, Hawaii and Alabama, still require a woman to take her husband's name on the marriage day.

The women's liberation movement ushered in a new form of address as well as a radical change in women's lives. The term "Ms." (pronounced MIZ) was introduced to substitute for Miss and Mrs. and to serve as effectively for women as "Mr." does for men. Ms. is generally used only in correspondence. We have not quite gotten around to saying "Miz Jones" or "Miz Brown" as a general thing.

Perhaps the most unusual example of the effect of women's liberation upon names is shown by Ellen Cooperman—oops, Cooper*person.* Ms. Cooperperson felt that her old name, Cooperman, was one more example of the way the word "man" in some form or another has always overshadowed our language. (Mankind, chairman, and manly have come under the gun, too.) She paid $350 to become Ellen Cooperperson—a lot of money to spend for feminine rights and to break the traditions of the English language.

A Phoenix, Arizona, woman kept her own name but named her little daughter Era. Era stands for the initials ERA, Equal Rights Amendment, the bill in Congress giving women greater equality. Maybe when Era grows up, she will dislike her name and change it to Rocmon (*R*ight *o*f *C*hanging *M*y *O*ld *N*ame)!

There is a storm brewing about naming hurricanes with feminine names like Hazel. Women feel that it is an insult to imply
that only females carry on like hurricanes. So hurricane Hazel is
giving way to hurricane Henri. Another small victory for women.

While some women are creating new name traditions for
themselves, another segment of society prefers to do as it has
always done. The Catholic Church continues age-old traditions
in naming. Priests entering the church usually change their
names. Priests and nuns leave behind all earthly goods, their
names too, and have new raiment for both their bodies and their
identities.

Let us take John Kelly. He becomes Brother James upon
entering a religious order. He has given up his name as surely as
he has given up his old life and dedicated his new one to God.
In Biblical times, early Christians sometimes changed their
names. Simon became known as Peter, and Saul became Paul.
The name change helped them to focus on a new life devoted
to God.

A Catholic boy or girl about to be confirmed has the happy
opportunity of choosing the name of a saint as a middle name.
At Confirmation, in fifth or sixth grade, each boy and girl adopts
a new and saintly name. Ruth Ann Lynch becomes Ruth Ann
Monica Lynch. Thomas Szonntagh lengthens his name to
Thomas Gabriel Szonntagh.

Perhaps you are a Catholic and have had fun looking up
your name in a book of saints. There is a special patron saint for
almost every day of the year, a saint to watch over persons in
most occupations, and certain saints to help sick people.

If your name is Monica, you have a name rich in meaning.
Monica is the patron saint of wives and mothers. St. Monica is
much admired because of her importance to the family. Most
girls who bear the name Monica are familiar with the picture of
her standing beside her kneeling son St. Augustine.

A child named Christopher often takes his name from the
beloved St. Christopher. This holy man is said to have carried the
Christ-child across a stream on his shoulders.

Middle names, juniors, surnames, name changes—there are

so many aspects to the name game. Traditions and current trends play an important part. And although naming still lies largely with the parents, Miss X and Master Y are injecting their own thoughts on the subject too.

12 *All About Nicknames*

Parents think long and hard about naming a child, hoping to find a name that cannot be shortened or changed.

But there are very few names that cannot be "nicknamed." Mother or Dad may decide on the name Brian if it's a boy, Karen for a girl. There's no way you can change Brian, the parents announce triumphantly. What can you do with Karen? You certainly can't add a *y* as you do with Patty or Jimmy. Kareny and Briany would sound pretty silly.

But as soon as Brian has schoolmates, they will figure out something to do with his name. Perhaps he will be called Bri (pronounced like tie). Karen is likely to become Kari when she settles into a circle of friends.

Yes, just about every name can be nicknamed. Do you have a nickname? You probably do, because people have a tendency to play around with a name until they feel comfortable with it. Jeffrey is bound to become Jeff, and Jennifer, Jen. And even if the first name doesn't readily yield a nickname, the last name probably will.

Then here is another situation. A parent may choose a child's name especially for the nickname that can be made from it. If a mother has always fancied Babby or Babs for a girl, she will name her daughter Barbara. (Babs, Babby, Barby, and Bobbie are among the many nicknames for Barbara.) So Babby it is, until maybe age eleven, when suddenly she feels she would prefer her formal name. It's so much more "grown-up." Mother is out of luck. With Babby gone, the daughter has a name that Mom really hadn't planned on using.

Nicknames spring up for many reasons. Baby talk is one of

them. A little girl who can't get her tongue around a big name like Elizabeth may settle for calling herself Beth. Tad from Theodore, Jodie from Julia, and Tina—short for Christina—and other shortened forms of names are often the result of little people trying to pronounce big names.

As we mentioned before, some of these shortened forms have become accepted as full names over the years. Betty, Kate, Bert, and Harry are quite common names for birth certificates today.

Then, just as the boys and girls begin to approach adulthood and perhaps formalize their names by dropping nicknames, they begin to use name baby talk again. That's because they're in love! At least the silly love names they choose for the favorite young man or woman in their life sound like baby talk. A sampling: Acorn, Angelfish, Budgie, Bunnyfluff, Sweetie Pie, Cuddles, Snufkin, and Honey Pot. Don't laugh—someday, you'll find the perfect (and perfectly silly) name for someone you like.

Nicknames go back a long way. Can you believe that the nickname of an important Roman consul five hundred years before Christ was Stupid? Or that in 2600 B.C., the pet name of an Egyptian was engraved inside his tomb? Pepiseshemsenefer was called Senni for short (no wonder!), and his survivors wanted to include his nickname in his burial place.

Nicknames arose in the many centuries before surnames made their appearance. Nicknames served a valuable purpose because they helped to keep members of a household with the same name separate from one another.

Today, nicknames are popular in countries around the world. In Russia, for instance, a little girl can be top-heavy with nicknames. Russians adore their children and shower them with affectionate names. South American countries, such as Argentina, also have special pet names for their children. The names below sound like happy jingles:

BOYS: Tito, Lito, Fito, Pepe, Pepito, Chicho, Quini, Lucho, Beto,   Quique, Cacho, Cachito, Carlitos, Pirincho, Pancho, Panchito,

Mingo, Tato
GIRLS: Pichuca, Pichona, Tuca, Ñata, Chata,
Mecha, Tita, Lita, Kequi,   Pepita, Chicha,
Chocha, Chuchi, Cuca, Tina, Chela, Negrita,
Pelusita

Some people famous in the sports world, the arts, and political fields are better known by their nicknames than by their real names. Who has ever heard of George Hamilton Ruth? But Babe Ruth? Of course. And Theodore Seuss Geisel? He is Dr. Seuss of *Cat in the Hat* fame. Doc is a nickname for quite a few other celebrities.

United States Presidents have had nicknames both beloved and derogatory. Honest Abe Lincoln, Teddy Roosevelt, Ike Eisenhower, and, of course, Jimmy Carter, instead of the more formal James Earl Carter. President Carter chose the informal Jimmy because he felt that he could appeal more effectively to his fellow citizens if he had a friendly-sounding first name. Richard Thornburgh, when inaugurated as governor of Pennsylvania in 1979, decided to follow Mr. Carter's lead and call himself Dick. He announced that he would be Dick Thornburgh for speeches, ceremonies, and general politicking.

Dick and Jimmy may have started something new, but what they gain in friendliness they may lose in dignity.

Many people in American history have had nicknames. Famous people were often nicknamed according to their reputations. Benjamin Franklin was dubbed the Tamer of Lightning because he was a scientist-inventor. The high opinion that Louis XIV of France had of himself was reflected in his nickname, The Sun King.

Sometimes individuals were singled out for one unusual deed—or misdeed. Society was sure to label them with an appropriate nickname. Joseph Moody, as a young man of the 1700's, accidentally killed a comrade with a gun. He was so grief-stricken that whenever he appeared in public he covered his face with a handkerchief. Joseph became known as Handkerchief Moody, and he never recovered from the tragic accident.

Persons prominent in politics often inherit names that have

to do with their former occupations. Thomas Metcalfe, a politician in the late eighteenth century, was called Old Stone Hammer because as a young man he was a stonemason and builder. And Honest Abe Lincoln was also nicknamed the Rail-splitter, because he split fence rails as a youth to earn money to study law.

George W. Connally had a funny nickname—Rubber Arm. He was a major-league baseball pitcher in the early 1900's and could go right into a game without warming up. This meant that he was in great shape and his pitching arm was as elastic as a rubber band.

Some nicknames focus on locale. Marie Ahnighito Peary, born to the Arctic explorer's wife during an expedition when the explorer hoped to reach the North Pole was called Snow Baby by the natives. The fortunate Admiral Peary gained a new daughter as well as international fame. The White Mountain Giant, E. A. Crawford, was nearly as massive as that great mountain range in New Hampshire. He was almost seven feet tall, and his dizzying height and enormous strength earned him this picturesque nickname.

Mary Todd Lincoln, President Lincoln's wife, had a very bad temper. History books say that she was often called the She-wolf. It was rumored that she chased her husband out of their house with a broomstick and once threw a bucket of water out of the window as he knocked at the front door begging to come in. Her terrible temper was often triggered by severe headaches. Headaches can be unbearable, so perhaps Mary Todd Lincoln's nickname, She-wolf, was a bit harsh.

In the late 1800's, the children in Oswego, New York, had a wonderful friend. They named him the Ain't-Gonna-Rain-No-Mo' Man because he gave the youngsters picnics under cloudless skies for nearly fifty years. No, he didn't "order" sunny days. But it is not surprising that the weather was on the side of such a kind person.

Perhaps you have a favorite older lady or gentleman friend in your neighborhood who always serves hot cider on Halloween night or takes you to the library for an armload of books. It may well be that you have given him or her a kindly nickname.

Some people are so famous that they have a whole slew of nicknames. We know George Washington as the Father of Our Country. But he has also been called:

The Atlas of America
The Deliverer of America
The Farmer-President
The Father of America
The Father of Pittsburgh
The Old Fox
The Sage of Mount Vernon
The Savior of Our Country
The Surveyor President
The Sword of the Revolution

It is obvious that he was a father many times over, although he had no children of his own. Many of these names must have been used only in his lifetime, because they are unfamiliar to us.

Nicknames for a celebrity today highlight what is special, just as they always have. Bobby Fischer, the chess champion, is the Corduroy Killer because he wore corduroy during his chess games. Frank Sinatra is called The Voice or Old Blue Eyes by fans both old and new. Pope John Paul I was known as the Smiling Pope. Newspaper photographs around the world showed a beaming, friendly man.

There is another segment of society that favors nicknames. In the shadowy world of crime, nicknames are as plentiful as holdups. These names are also known as "aliases." Jack Carver, who signs into a motel with plans to burglarize the rooms, may have a "tool kit" of other names or aliases when he plans to ply his trade elsewhere.

Did you know that the FBI has a nickname file for criminals? In it are 150,000 very colorful names. The files help the FBI to trace down Gold Tooth or Bugsy. Within the criminal underworld, shady characters are known simply by these inventive names. Last names are not safe to use, and a highly descriptive first name like Scarface is easy to remember.

The criminal may accept—even be proud of—his or her

nickname. But for many other people such informal names may not always be desirable. "Sticks and stones may break my bones, but names will never hurt me" is not necessarily true. Unkind nicknames can hurt.

How do some of these unkind nicknames come about? They are often chosen to describe the way a person looks or acts. Fatty Chandler and Scaredy-Cat Johnson are hard names to live down. Unpleasant nicknames that come from a given name are no better. Slobby Bobby and Betsy Wetsy really need help. Very bright children often get labeled Computer, Robot, or Freak. If you have friends or acquaintances with such "tags," call them by their correct name. A boy stuck with a hurtful nickname may be so miserable that he would trade it in for a case of poison ivy.

And if you have a nickname you hate, what can you do about it? Like a bad cold, it may go away if you follow this prescription:

1. If your nickname really does describe you, try to do something about it. Fatty Chandler will probably regain her normal name if she slims down.

2. Ignore the name. Don't play to the crowd by showing your annoyance. If people can't get a rise out of you, they may quit. After all, making you miserable was half the fun. If you won't play the game, they may get tired of it.

3. If you are the butt of many unkind nicknames, take a good look at yourself. Is there something about you that is turning your peers off? A visit to a school counselor or a query to a classroom teacher may give you some ideas on how you can pick up new acceptance—and a nice new nickname to go with it.

Many nicknames are happy names and people like to have them. Posie, Flossie, Cherie, and Missy are pet names that seem to suit the people who have them. Chuck, Red, or Buzz may substitute for more formal names throughout a lifetime. Nicknames are welcome additions when they bring pleasure instead of pain to their owners.

13 *Hiding Behind a Made-up Name*

Have you ever wanted to leave your signature off something you have written? You preferred to keep your work anonymous, or unsigned. Perhaps you criticized the cafeteria food in the school newspaper or wrote an essay for English class called "Why My Teacher Is Boring." Your opinions were interesting but perhaps a bit risky. Professional writers have felt this way, too. Because of this, they have often adopted pen names. A pen name is a substitute name that allows an author to conceal his or her real identity.

When a writer hides behind a pen name or a pseudonym, that person has strong reasons for remaining unknown. Daniel Defoe, author of *Robinson Crusoe,* had many political enemies to deal with. To escape their wrath, he signed some of his pieces Eye Witness. George Eliot's real name was Mary Ann Evans. She used her pen name, a man's name, to write *Silas Marner* because the nineteenth century frowned on female writers. It wasn't lady-like to be an author.

Just as Alice, in the book *Alice's Adventures in Wonderland,* swallowed a magic potion that made her smaller, the English author Lewis Carroll "swallowed" his real name, Charles Lutwidge Dodgson, and chose to sign his famous stories with his pen name. As Dodgson, he was a professor of mathematics; as Lewis Carroll, he was a teller of tall tales. The secretive photographer-writer didn't want his college students and friends to know of his literary talent. He wished to remain Professor Dodgson, lecturer in mathematics at Oxford University.

What would you use for your pen name? If you are a tall and lanky boy, maybe The Thin Man would amuse and confuse. A

Alice in Wonderland
by
~~Charles Lutwidge Dodgson~~
Lewis Carroll

young lady with a mind of her own and a sense of fair play could be The Conscience.

Code names as well as pen names are used to conceal identity. Code names are not necessarily in code form, but they are meant to hide the sender's identity as fully as possible. Duckpin, General Eisenhower's code name, and Admiral Q, President Franklin Roosevelt's alias, are certainly amusing substitutes for these famous names. But code names were not assigned to important people for lighthearted purposes. When it was necessary to disguise General Eisenhower as the source of military moves in World War II, it was Duckpin who gave the secret orders rather than the General. This prevented the enemy from connecting certain war plans with the Supreme Commander.

It doesn't seem unusual to substitute one name for another for literary or military protection. But several people have decided that they prefer numbers for names!

Michael Dengler of Minneapolis, Minnesota, decided to rename himself 1069. But as Mr. 1069, he was soon in deep trouble. When he disposed of his name, he also lost his teaching job and his telephone and gas service. The principal of the high school where he taught probably thought the pupils would break up when they said, "Good morning, Mr. 1069!"

Numbers are as cold and colorless as names, yet they are being used increasingly as name substitutes. Perhaps that's why Michael Dengler had so much trouble. He represents a trend that many people don't like. He is a number, not a man.

Take John Jones. Even though he keeps his name, he is just a number to his bank, another to the Bureau of Motor Vehicles, and another to any other impersonal organization that wants to computerize him. He is not officially John Jones. For one thing, he is 128–62–7435 (his Social Security number). As 694830 (his bank account number) he withdraws money from the bank. And there he goes as 8492D (driver's license number), whizzing down the street in his new Mustang. But not for long. Now he is 62810, newly inducted into the Armed Forces. The last thing he needs is a number for a formal name.

Prisoners live in a world of numbers, too. They are assigned a number the minute they walk through the prison door. You can bet they are glad to get back to being just a name when they have served their sentence!

On the lighter side, though, census records reveal a Willie ⅝ Smith and a Mr. 54°40'. The latter's very precise "fifty-four degrees, forty minutes" name was influenced by the battle over Oregon territory in 1846 to settle the boundary between Oregon country and British northwest possessions.

Love-22 was a 1978 Presidential candidate (even though it was not an election year) for the Independent Love Party. He chose his name on the basis of a system of numerical values for letters in the alphabet.

Love-22, an amiable fellow in a red, white, and blue outfit, passed out fake $22 bills and chanted, "A vote for love is a vote for you, yaba, daba, doo, twenty-two, twenty-two." It is doubtful that Love-22 received many votes, but at least he livened up the political scene.

Numbers as names seem very uninteresting. But numbers play another role in naming that makes them quite fascinating.

From ancient times, numbers have been assigned to names to forecast a baby's future. Pythagoras, the Greek philosopher and mathematician, felt that numbers had good and bad vibes— a slang word we use today to mean feelings.

Numerologists give a number to each letter of the alphabet. Every letter in a person's name, then, has a certain number. By combining the numbers assigned to each name in a certain way, the numerologist predicts whether life will be rough or smooth in that person's future. But few of these number philosophers agree on what combinations to use for their fortune-telling, so numerology is not an exact science.

14 *Name Fame*

John Henry . . . Pecos Bill . . . Davy Crockett . . . Paul Bunyan
. . . Wrong-Way Corrigan . . . Florence Nightingale.

Most people—and their names—disappear with time. But actions of some men and women keep history or legend alive, and their names are instantly recognizable. "He's as strong as John Henry," you will hear. Or, "She's a regular Florence Nightingale," referring to a woman who patiently nursed someone back to health. "Put your John Hancock on this," and with a flourish you sign your name—not John Hancock's. Hancock signed the Declaration of Independence in big, bold letters so that King George III of England "could read it without his spectacles."

The Real McCoy—the honest-to-goodness product, not a fake—is an expression arising from Elijah McCoy's automatic lubricating system of 1880. Meat suppliers of that time wanted to make sure they were getting the Real McCoy and not an imitation of the cooling system that revolutionized the meat industry.

Many of the people with "bigger than life" names were large in stature too. Perhaps it takes a tall man to weave a tall story. Paul Bunyan, the giant hero of the American Northwest, was said to have a blue ox named Babe that measured forty-two ax handles and a plug of chewing tobacco between the horns. And Bunyan's logging camp adventures were reported as outsized as he. (He dug Puget Sound, it is said!) His counterpart in the Southwest, Pecos Bill, was so big he "staked out New Mexico and fenced Arizona for a calf pasture," according to legend. Another tall tale has it that when the water got scarce on Bill's range, he

dug the Rio Grande River and fed water in from the Gulf of Mexico!

Another legendary character, John Henry, was a "steel-drivin' man," according to the song that celebrates his skill and strength at railroad-building.

If these names stand for legendary adventure, Wrong-Way Corrigan is a nickname that was earned for a strange, real-life event that made headlines at the time.

On July 17, 1938, newspapers around the United States recorded the strange flight of a thirty-one-year-old pilot, Douglas Corrigan. Corrigan flew from New York to Baldomel, Ireland, but he claimed he was really headed for California! His Curtiss Robin aircraft had no radio and few instruments to guide him. It is quite possible that he thought he was heading west instead of eastward across the Atlantic Ocean.

Many products are named after the persons who invented or marketed them. In automobiles alone, the list is impressive: Buick, Dodge, Chrysler, Ford, and Oldsmobile. The British MG is named for a person too. MG stands for Morris Garages, the company formed by Mr. Morris to make his little cars. The Morgan was named for its maker Peter Morgan.

Among American cars, one—Chevrolet—was named for a racing driver. And one man in automotive history put his name on two cars. Ransome E. Olds first made the Oldsmobile. When he sold his interest in Oldsmobile, he sold the use of his name as well. Later, after he decided to reenter the automobile market, he used his initials to make and sell REO cars and trucks.

Other products named after their manufacturers or inventors are the Land camera, the Murphy bed, the Franklin stove (invented by Ben himself), Westinghouse and Maytag appliances, and Du Pont chemical products. There is the reverse idea, too. Products are now named after fictitious people or are contrived names: Mr. Clean, Mr. Coffee, and Sara Lee.

There is someone so famous that he appears frequently in articles and in important papers such as job applications and income tax returns. He is fictitious, too. His name is John Doe and he is Mr. Anybody, U.S.A.

His name is used to represent a typical person in newspaper articles: "John Doe is now working a 44-hour week." Or, "Statistics show that John Doe owns 1.6 cars."

But John Doe gets a real workout when it comes to forms.

```
         J O H N   D O E
_____
NAME  3 8
_____
AGE   S A L E S M A N
_____
EXPERIENCE
```

Poor John Doe! Because he isn't real, his name is usually written in a broken line on applications and forms. But then it seems right that this fictitious gentleman appears on paper in such a ghostly way. His wife is equally shadowy—

```
         J A N E   D O E
```

A very inventive group of people are not satisfied to leave names to history. Five thousand Americans and Canadians have banded together to adopt medieval names and relive the exciting days of the Middle Ages. They get together and joust across the fields in armor and chain mail. The lady members play their part, too. Dressed in long gowns, they spin and sew just as the ladies did in the long-ago days of King Arthur.

Each member chooses a knightly name to match his new role in life. Michael Peterson of Rockford, Illinois, has recast himself as Halfden Greenleaf, a fine old English name. And that's the name you will find in the phone book. Anyone can call him up to make an appointment—for a duel.

Some American families jousted for wealth and power long before today's knights in armor thought of jousting for fun. Those who won did so in a big way. Their names are legend because their fabulous backgrounds have put them in the public eye.

"Rich as Rockefeller" is a fairly common expression, and a line in a popular song. Rockefeller, Vanderbilt, Du Pont, and Mellon are important names because they represent families that have made great fortunes. Families like these have donated large sums of money to charity and research.

Each family had its own way of building its fortune. The Mellons' success came about at the end of the nineteenth century after they invested a sum of money in a small business that produced aluminum. Today they are one of America's largest aluminum manufacturers, and tycoons in other businesses. The Du Ponts, arriving in the late 1700's from France, were wealthy to begin with. Their friends included such famous men as President Thomas Jefferson. It was Jefferson who persuaded Irénée Du Pont to open a gunpowder factory. This enterprise brought in millions—millions that were reinvested in other businesses. Today, Du Pont is far better known for chemical products than for explosives.

John D. Rockefeller controlled 90 percent of America's oil in the 1880's. His children and his children's children used much of their great wealth to help others. Their name today crowns building complexes and institutions. The Rockefeller Institute for Medical Research and the Rockefeller Foundation are two examples of Rockefeller generosity.

There are other people whose names mean money, too. They are not as "rich as Rockefeller," but they have enough money to share it with others in a very unusual way. These persons have set up scholarships for any students bearing their names. At Harvard University, for instance, needy students named Murphy can accept financial aid, thanks to a wealthy college alumnus, William Stanislaus Murphy.

Someday *you* may want to leave money to a student who shares your last name.

15 *T. Hee and Other Odd Names*

Mr. T. Hee of Los Angeles, California, made people laugh. For years he spun tall yarns for Walt Disney Studios. T. Hee was an excellent name for a comedy writer.

But not all funny names are fun to live with. The names Tonsilitis and Appendicitis, given to two children of an Oklahoma couple, may have been a laugh to their classmates, but living with such names was probably more painful than the medical problems after which the children were named. Tonsilitis, incidentally, finally had his tonsils removed in 1955 after he had grown up.

Many other odd names seem to belong in comic strips, but real people walk around with them. "That's right, I'm Mr. Sillyman," one gentleman replies. "Yes, this is Mrs. Boozy," the lady says, answering the phone. "This is Mr. Vroom speaking. Your motorcycle is repaired. You can pick it up anytime."

Candy Barr and Dill Pickle would seem to be two persons who shouldn't meet. But their names may not describe their personalities.

Most odd names have nothing to do with the meaning that first comes to mind. Mr. Sillyman is not silly; his name has gradually changed over the years from Seeleyman and Sealyman to Sillyman. There is no explanation for the gradual changes of names and words except that many of our ancestors were not always careful about spelling, and others could not read at all.

The name Smellie is a variation of Smalley, a small English town. It means Small Lea—Smel-lie—a small, enclosed area. Miss Sneezum pronounces her name like the good old-fashioned "Aachoo!" because that is the way Snettisham, in Norfolk, England, was once pronounced. Snet—now Sneez—means Wise. Mr. Muddyman is not a man all covered with mud. Muddy means Moody in this case.

Very long names are as noticeable as odd names. Do you have friends with long last names—names with ten or eleven letters? The last name of a policeman in Polynesia has 130 letters! It's Marika Tuimudremudrenicagitokalaunatobakonatewa-enagaunakalakivolaikoyakinakotamanaenaiivolanikawabualena-valenivolavolaniyasanamaisomosomo. This long name tells the story of a voyage Marika's father made to register his son's name with the proper officials.

Other long names often tell stories, too. No one has yet named a child Abcdefghijklmnopqrstuvwxyz, but it could happen. Or, if parents want to indicate that their child is going to be bright, they can name him or her Encyclopedia. Famous book character Encyclopedia Brown, boy detective, takes on such exciting challenges as tracking down the marbles thief at the big marbles tournament.

Slogans and expressions do not often include personal names. But one name was heard and seen everywhere during World War II. "Kilroy Was Here" appeared in the strangest places—scrawled in paint across park benches, traced in the sand with a shell, sprayed on bathroom mirrors with shaving cream.

"Kilroy Was Here" was popular during the pre-graffiti days. It came to mean any American soldier anywhere. Scrawled in a town occupied by the enemy or scribbled on a bar counter in the United States, it was the soldier's signature. But strangely enough, "Kilroy" eventually came to mean a very unimportant person. Poor Kilroy went from soldier to shadow.

A Philadelphia man, Burnap (pronounced bur-NAP) Post, found that he was called everything *but* Burnap. Letters were addressed to him as Turnip Post, Burnip Post, Burner Post, but seldom Burnap Post. He decided to cut out the incorrect spellings from the envelopes and paste them in a little notebook. Soon he had a whole book full.

Burnap was a prominent last name in Mr. Post's family.

Daniel Burnap was a New England clockmaker who kept clocks ticking all around the town of Andover, Connecticut. Burnap Post's parents liked the idea of giving their son a family name with so much tradition.

Burnap has always liked his name, but he finds it hard to get people to spell it right. After receiving close to forty pieces of misspelled mail, he was amused by a letter that had a post office stamp stating: "No Such Person Exists." The letter had Mr. Post's name spelled *right!*

Here are the many ways Burnap has been spelled by his business acquaintances and friends: Ernest, Burner, Burnao, Burnard, Bert, Berle, Barns, Burned, Bernup, Burnep, Burnam, Burnip, Purnett, Burnan, Burnys, Burlap, Burnett, Baynip, Rubnap, Burnape, Burnapp, Bernee, Berap, Bunap, Burna, Bernhap, Burham, Belknap, Burknap, Bunrap, Burnpa, Burnab, Bumat-Post, Barnat, Burnat, Bernat, Bernap, Barnap, Buxnap, Biernap, Buinap, Brunap, Belnap, Durnap, Gernap, Nurnap, Burnt, Bornap, Burnop, and Bunny.

And, says Mr. Post, those who do spell his first name right fall down on his last name. This is because the effort to spell Burnap correctly has been too great! He cites Burnap Oost, Burnap Pots, and Burnap Fost as examples. Mr. Post's name may have been a burden to him, but at least it gives him a hobby— name-collecting his own name!

Names can get changed around, as Mr. Post well knows. A slip of the pen or a slip of the tongue and a perfectly ordinary name becomes an odd one. A young lady named Anita had lived with this problem for a long time when she wrote to Ann Landers:

> Dear Ann Landers:
>
> My parents named me Anita. The person who wrote out the birth certificate misspelled my name and it came out "Anutta." When I started school I had to bring my birth certificate. Since it read "Anutta," my mother felt certain I was stuck with it so that's what everybody called me. Naturally, I was "nut" for short.

I hated the name but neither my parents nor anyone else believed anything could be done about it, so I remained "Anutta."

I'm 20 now and just learned something that might help others, although it's too late for me.

Anyone who wants his or her first name corrected (or changed) on a birth certificate can do so for a small fee. Here's how: write to the Vital Records section of the Department of Public Health in the city of your birth. Proper forms will be sent to be filled out. The notarized signature of the parent, older relative, or friend is all that is needed.—New Name

Dear New Name: It's not too late for you. Get rid of the "nut" and be "neat" as in Anita.

(From The Philadelphia Inquirer. Used by permission of the Field Newspaper Syndicate.)

Misspellings on a birth certificate can cause problems later in life. The person who doesn't want to go through the bother of correcting the certificate has to use the spelling for all sorts of identification. If the baby nurse is careless when reporting infant Mark's name to the Bureau of Vital Statistics, he might come out as Bark on the birth certificate. In five or six years he could be fighting with pals who learned of this little error and made barking sounds for their amusement.

Most persons' names are spelled correctly on the birth certificate. But some choose to be difficult about their names and create problems where none exist. A man whose first name was Llewellyn took it as a personal insult if his name was misspelled. Llewellyn, a Welsh name, has various accepted spellings. Lewelyn and Llewelyn are other ways of spelling this fine old name. But for this particular Llewellyn, it had to be four l's and nothing else. A niece invited him to a wedding, writing "Dear Uncle Lewellyn—" That did it. "Dear Uncle Llewellyn" refused to attend the wedding. If his niece could not spell his name correctly, she obviously did not want him at the ceremony.

Pandora is a pretty name. It is neither strange nor difficult to pronounce. But a parent might think twice before giving a child this name. Apparently the parents of English-born Pandora Green did not. This small miss will have her hands full when she and her classmates study mythology. The original Pandora, you see, was a bad girl. Even though forbidden, she opened a box containing all the temptations in the world. Out flew greed, envy, and all the other miseries that we contend with today. After the lesson, Miss Pandora Green may wish she could put her name in a box and close the lid tightly!

Actors and actresses often have very unusual names, too. And they want to see these unusual names in big print. When their names go up on a movie or theater marquee, they want them higher and bigger than anyone else's name. And if the billing doesn't suit them, they may refuse to be in a play or movie.

Some persons feel strongly about their names for reasons other than correct spelling and size on a theater marquee. The poet e. e. cummings insisted that his name be spelled in small letters. Born Edward Estlin Cummings, cummings wanted to find new freedom in writing his poetry. He ignored rules of grammar and punctuation and sometimes ran words and sentences together.   itwasonlynaturalthatthewriterofsuchpoetrywouldsignhimselfe.e.cummings!

cummings was a man with a familiar, easy-to-spell name. Other people with simple names seldom have problems with them. That is why hopeful Hollywood and television stars have traded in complicated or harsh-sounding names for catchy and easily pronounceable ones. This is a rule of success for most aspiring actors and actresses.

But for every rule there is almost always an exception. Somewhere out there is someone who is deliberately changing his or her name to something very complicated or unusual. And memorable. Engelbert Humperdinck, the pop singer, was once plain old Arnold Dorsey. But Engelbert felt that Arnold Dorsey had so little pizzazz that he would never make it in the competitive world of singing. He chose the name of the composer of the children's opera *Hansel and Gretel* and became Engelbert Humperdinck—and a star.

Arnold Dorsey chose a fancier name. Linda Sano of Minneapolis reasoned much the same way. But she didn't trade in her simple name for a more flowery one. What she did do was to add on a few other names. Ten to be exact. Linda Elizabeth Zeamygk Xylona Opaline Zerdali Drusilla Holly Clare Sakura Kim Sano. To keep her "collection" straight, she tapes her names over her fireplace so she can memorize them.

Eugene Jerome Dupuis's children have a different challenge. They all have the same name! In a 1979 letter to Ann Landers, a reporter checking into the Dupuis household verified the existence of *six* juniors—three of them girls.

Writers of books about names often have very unusual ones themselves. Perhaps they have elected to write about names because their own have stirred interest in the subject. Leslie (a man) Dunkling, Linwood Sleigh, Florence Doody, Muriel Beadle, Edward Clodd, and Elizabeth G. Withycombe delved into the history and meaning of names. Withycombe mentions that Professor Onions helped her with her research. But perhaps the most surprising example of an unusual name for a writer is one that seems to contradict his subject matter. The book *The Crime Problem* is written by Walter Reckless!

Mary Price Lee, the author of this book, has a commonplace name. But before she married she was Mary Lys Price (Lys is the old French spelling for Lily). Her unusual name qualifies her as an oddly named author in search of other strange names.

The Burnaps and Llewellyns, Engelberts and Archibalds all bear names that enrich our language and reflect our heritage. Toms, Dicks and Harrys, Jans, Janes and Joans also people our world. It is nice to have both the hard names and the easy ones. And this is the way it will always be. For every thousand parents who decide on Bob or Mary, there will be a couple who won't be able to resist naming their child after an eclipse of the sun or the latest natural food herb!

16 *Naming Your Pets and Stuffed Animals*

Family cats and dogs always have names. But why stop with these familiar household pets? It is fun to give names to all kinds of live-in companions. Why not name a pet gerbil, a canary, or even a zebra fish?

A zebra fish is a pretty creature with lots of personality. It darts through the water, its stripes flashing in the lighted aquarium. This sea denizen could rightly be called Arrow because it moves very quickly. Or because of its horizontal striping it could be dubbed Prison Stripes or Z.B. for zebra.

Jean Taggart, who wrote *Pet Names,* came up with these suggestions for the little zebra fish. She has hundreds of other pet-name ideas for animals, birds, fish, and even insects. Her names catch the color and spirit of the animal kingdom. Nutmeg and Silver Lass, Wildflower and Bed o' Roses, Cockatoo and Limelight are names as colorful as the different animals they identify.

Mrs. Taggart has some nice ideas about *how* to name a pet, too. She suggests that you find a name by observing what your pet does best. If you have a Newfoundland dog, call it Tobias (meaning He of the Fish) in honor of its talent for fishing. Your new gerbil may like to hop from one level to another in its roomy cage. An appropriate name for the gerbil might be Jump Up.

Small pets need small names. Your pet spider can be Legs. Whir suits a hummingbird because its tiny wings beat faster than the eye can blink. Walter will do fine for a pigeon. The pigeon, a soft, cooing bird, will share his name with the actor Walter Pidgeon.

In 1978, a pet dove endured several different names. Lisa

and Marc Melaragni named their dove Menachem **Begin** when the Israeli prime minister began peace negotiations with Egypt. No peace treaty was made, so the dove was renamed Oscar after Oscar the Grouch in *Sesame Street.*

When the Israeli-Egyptian peace treaty was finally signed in 1979, Oscar the dove became Menachem Begin again.

If you live on a farm, you may have a whole zoo of animals. Perhaps you enjoy naming them as each one makes its arrival and adds to the barnyard bustle. Soon you will agree that there is no cow quite like Moo-Cow, no pony as gentle as Sweet Potato. Wilbur, whom you name after the pig in *Charlotte's Web,* and Billie-G, the billy goat, count on you for their daily meal. Farm animals with names are more than barnyard animals. They are friends. They come to you when you call their names.

Jean Taggart also suggests names for your ant, monkey, mouse, catfish, duck—even your seahorse! But before you look for help, try to think up a name of your own. The pet that you yourself name is apt to mean more to you.

We know where our friends live and what families they belong to. With animals, it is different. A cinnamon-flecked pussycat with a big fluffy tail may suddenly appear at a back door. Friends discover two orphaned wild baby rabbits nestled in the ivy. Lost, abandoned creatures are commonplace in the animal world.

There are two problems to be faced with these orphans: getting parents' permission to keep them and deciding upon a name. A photograph in a small-town newspaper showed a young girl and her newly found kitten, Struggle. The name of this young wanderer shows the owner's awareness of the kitten's recent struggle to survive.

The loving yet aloof, prowling yet contented cat has names to capture its varied personality. Cat Friendly, owned by a rural Pennsylvania apartment dweller, is just that. Sneaky, a neighbor of Friendly's, lives up to the name by catching unsuspecting birds. The Siamese or Thai cat, a feline "aristocat," needs a name to match its sleek, haughty appearance. Chantra sounds suitably exotic for the honey-colored Siamese.

Stuffed animals and wooden animal toys get names, too. "See this wooden lion? His name is Waldo 'cause he looks like he'd like that name," says a youngster with a roomful of play animals. "And that cloth elephant is Purple Mountain Majesty from 'America the Beautiful' 'cause he's bright purple."

There must be something special about bears. Three bears "most likely to succeed" in a stuffed animal contest are Teddy Bear, Winnie the Pooh, and Paddington Bear.

But the last two would have to bow to Teddy's greater popularity. This cuddly, arm-filling fellow has an interesting history. President Theodore Roosevelt, better known as Teddy Roosevelt, enjoyed hunting as relaxation after strenuous weeks in the White House. One day when his hunt produced nothing more than a squirrel and a rabbit, a bear cub was brought to Roosevelt's camp for the President to shoot. He declined, saying that the bear did not have the chance to defend itself.

This sportsmanlike act was later cartooned in the newspapers. One man, Morris Michtom, seeing the cartoon, suggested to his wife that she make a few stuffed bears like the one in the drawing. Rose Michtom whipped up three child-sized (two-and-a-half-foot) bears and placed them in the couple's candy store window. She rested a sign against their generous tummies that said "Teddy's Bears."

Soon people purchased the fuzzy bears. Mr. Michtom, delighted with the response, decided to write President Roosevelt and ask his permission to call the bears by the President's nickname. Roosevelt wrote back, commenting that he didn't feel that his name "would mean much to the toy bear business."

How wrong he was! Millions of teddy bears and a fortune earned for Michtom as well as for other toy companies have proved the presidential name to be a drawing card.

A teddy bear that decorates a little girl's room often stays around to go to college. When young Miss goes to the university, the now very worn but beloved stuffed animal goes along.

Teddy is plopped down on a dormitory bed and is forced to listen to hours of stereo music at top decibel while his mistress studies. But Teddy has his happier moments. He may go off to the classroom when his pretty companion takes an examination. You see, Teddy is her mascot. His presence is supposed to bring her good luck. No other bear will do, just this one-eyed, one-eared creature who has been with her almost forever. He is real to her. And part of his being real is that he has a name of his own.

17 *Name Games*

Names are serious. Names are fun. You can write a history book about them. Or you can play games with them. In this chapter, you will find some quizzes and riddles, all having to do with names. The chapter winds up with the biggest name game of them all, autograph-collecting.

Look-It-Up-Game. Lots of names begin with the same root. Take *good,* for instance. There are a whole slew of Goods in the telephone book. How many can you find? Now, how many names can you find *beginning* with Good? How many Goodmans? Goodyears? Any others? Try this game with names beginning with Black and Smith. (You will think of others.)

Song Title Game. Are there enough name songs for each letter of the alphabet? Almost! Some evening, play the song game with your family or friends, using first names as titles. Start the game off with a song name that begins with *A.* ("Sweet Adeline.") The person next to you must think of a *B* song. Among the best-known name songs of 1979 were "Peg," "Josie," "Caroline," "James," "Rosalita," and "Sandy." Perhaps you remember them. There are some good old oldies like "K-K-K-Katie" and "Lili" ("Hi, Lili, Hi, Lo"). Stealing from operas is fair game too. There is a treasure trove of names to be found in the great operas. *Monica, Carmen,* and *Vanessa* are just a beginning. Aaron Copland's *Billy the Kid* ballet should qualify in this name game.

Last-Letter Game. Let's say two of you are playing. You go first by giving a name—any name. Suppose you choose PATRICK.

97

Now your friend must choose a name *starting* with the last letter of the name you just gave. The friend says KIM. You respond with MARY. Keep on giving names. The first person who cannot give a name starting with the last letter of the previous name is the loser.

Word Lightning Names.   You will need a clock with a second hand for this one. A chosen leader points to any one player and calls out a letter. The target player calls out as many names as he or she can think of beginning with that letter. He continues thinking up names for one minute—until someone gives him the signal to stop. A scorer must be counting all the names. The scorer records the total. If the leader called out the letter *M,* the player would have one minute to come up with names such as "Margaret, Martin, Molly, Mary, Merry, Mitch, Mindy, Matilda . . . Bong!"

The first player now calls a letter to another person and the game continues. Some rules need to be established about what letters may be chosen. Some letters are easier than others for name-calling. After all, how many names beginning with *X, Y,* or *Z* are there!

A good way to solve this problem is to write all the letters of the alphabet (except for the uncommon ones) on separate pieces of paper. Then put the papers in a box and stir them around. Each player picks a slip of paper with a letter.

Name Ghost.   Ghost is a spelling game. Generally, in Ghost all words are allowed except proper nouns. In other words, no names. But with this game, *only* names are allowed (and no nicknames).

Any number of players can play Name Ghost. One player begins the game by thinking of any name of more than three letters and announcing the first letter of that name. The person next to the first player must now think of a name beginning with the given letter. It must be a name that has at least four letters. He or she gives the second letter, and then each player in turn adds on a letter with a specific name in mind. But there is one

catch to all this—no one must ever complete any name after the first three letters have been spelled out.

For instance, the first person calls out *P,* the second person offers *A,* and the third, *T.* Now we have three letters and the name PAT. But because it is all right to end a name in less than four letters, the game can go on. Letters are added right along, because everyone has PATRICIA or PATRICK in mind. The fourth person offers *R,* the fifth, *I,* the sixth, *C. K* would end the round and force the next player out, so the player adds *I.* This forces the next person to say *A.* She has now spelled PATRICIA and is a third of a ghost. If she loses a second time, she will be two thirds of a ghost. And a third time makes her a bona fide full ghost. When she has reached this state of unhappiness, she has lost and the game is over.

Name Stories.   Below are listed parts of Old English names and their meanings. Do you have any friends whose first names—either the beginnings or the ends of them—have one of these Old English word roots? Do your friends with these names fit the name descriptions?

OLD ENGLISH	MEANING	TODAY'S NAMES
Har	warrior or warfare	Harold
Rick or Ric	ruler or king	Richard, Eric
-rad or -red	counsel or wisdom	Conrad
-lind	serpent, smoothness	Rosalind, Linda

All names are words, words beginning with capitals. Jones. Lee. Rosemary. Murray. Some names have entered our language as everyday words and stand for things, actions, and places—instead of people. These names, first and last, are words without capitals.

Try making up a story with name words. Here is a sample story. Definitions for the more unfamiliar names are given below.

The *billy goat hectored* the *bobby* by chasing the pudgy officer across the *glen.* The *billy* was in fine shape for a race after consuming a tin can, a *louis,* a *dickey* from a lady's outfit, and a *jack-in-the-box.* They both ran like the *dickens.* A *robin* joined in the merry chase.

The poor *bobby* was getting a *charley horse* from all the running. Suddenly the roly-poly *bobby* fell, a *hank* of hair slipping from under his helmet. It looked as though a *derrick* or a *jack* might be needed to get the heavy fellow upright. But the *billy goat,* spotting a *sterling silver* officer's badge for his latest meal, tugged at the *bobby*'s jacket, and the *bobby* jumped up to save his badge.

> *bobby*—English policeman
> *charley horse*—a cramp in the muscles of the arm or leg
> *derrick*—a machine for hoisting or moving large objects
> *dickens* (. . . like the dickens)—fast, pursued by the devil
> *dickey*—a detachable collar or blouse front
> *glen*—narrow valley
> *hank*—a loop or coil of something flexible
> *hectored*—bothered
> *jack*—a hand-operated machine used to lift something
> *louis*—a French gold coin

Same-Name People. Your first name belongs to you. It also belongs to many other persons, some of them quite famous. The more common your name, the more famous namesakes you have. Check into the biographical index of your dictionary or the index of an encyclopedia and try to find as many famous persons as you can who share your name. Check encyclopedias and *Who's Who in America.* Not all the Johns or Marys you find will be famous for the right reasons. John Wilkes Booth shot Abraham Lincoln while the President sat watching a play. Mary, the lady pirate, disguised herself as a man and made a career of looting ships in the late eighteenth century. Other Johns and Marys have smudged history with their misdeeds.

But on the whole, bearers of these popular names have made great contributions to civilization. Five Johns signed the Declaration of Independence. John Cabot claimed Canada for the British. John Glenn made his claim in outer space.

Marys spice history with great dancers, athletes, and actresses. Maria Tallchief, an American Indian, is a famous ballerina. Mary Bacon is a well-known jockey, riding racetrack horses to victory. And Mary Martin, not too long ago, zoomed across the stage as the beloved Peter Pan.

So if you're a John or a Mary, you can find a lot about your name people. If your name is Gregory or Bernadette, you may have some digging to do. Ask your librarian to help you.

Collecting Autographs. This is the grandest name game of them all. Autographs are signatures. And signatures of famous men and women are considered very valuable. Autograph-collecting, like stamp- or coin-collecting, can be a very expensive and exciting hobby or profession. But not all autographs cost money. Signatures of friends or a collection of unusual names of persons you know can also be a wonderful hobby. Besides, it costs you nothing but time.

The nicknames, name changes, and royal names of history that you have read about crop up among the famous collectibles too. Mark Twain, whose autograph brings hundreds of dollars, preferred this sea term to his real name, Samuel Clemens. Babe Ruth liked his nickname and used his formal one only to sign checks.

The names of kings and queens are among the most famous collectible names in European history. While the lower classes were gradually adding last names to their given ones, monarchs retained single names. Autograph dealers are always searching for rare documents signed with a royal flourish by Queen Isabella of Spain or Henry VIII of England.

Scott Deindorfer is a pursuer of famous names. In fact, he has over two hundred and fifty signed autographs of celebrities with their favorite sayings.

"I have the world's greatest collection for an eleven-year-old," Scott says. His gallery of top names bolsters this claim.

Perhaps Scott had such luck because he had a smart idea for getting responses to his requests for autographs. He asked his idols to write their favorite sayings. Astronaut Buzz Aldrin wrote,

"No dream is too high for those with their eyes in the sky."

Perhaps you can think of an interesting approach to lure famous people into signing their names for you. Remember Buzz Aldrin's advice when you make your pitch: "No dream is too high . . ."

There are other kinds of autographs to collect. A pajama party or a camping trip is an opportunity to ask friends to sign a book and comment on their experiences. Boys and girls have autograph books with such immortal words as "Roses are red, Violets are blue, I am crazy and so are you," scribbled by best friends.

Perhaps you have an autograph book filled with names and messages of good friends. Someday you will flip through the pages and laugh at some of the funny things that are written in it, remembering old friends.

There are other kinds of autographs that you can collect too. You can divide an autograph book into sections and gather special names.

1. Collect amusing or unusual names. You may not be able to match Ima Hogg or U. Jerk, but is there someone in your town whose name is Toogood, or a store sign with the owner's name, Meet's Market or Peddle's Bike Shop?

2. Try to find names—perhaps those of neighbors—that would go together to tell a story: *Park* the *Carr* in front of the *House.* If you get Mr. Carr, Mr. Park, and Mr. House to sign your book, the results may look like this:

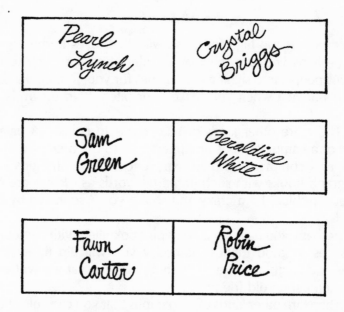

3. Find persons whose names are jewels, colors, animals, birds.

4. Collect names that represent occupations. Occupational surnames such as Miller and Weaver have their opposites in names that may (or may not) have inspired the men who had them—another name game to play. Did George Pullman invent the railroad sleeping car because he wanted a more comfortable way to *pull men* from one city to another? Did Alexander Graham Bell invent the telephone with its ringing *bell* because of his name? You might enjoy thinking of people you know whose last names reflect their interests, occupations, or abilities. Or you could have fun finding such names in the Yellow Pages. In Philadelphia, for instance, you will find a Glassman's Auto Glass, and not too many names away, there is Krakovitz Glass Company—a courageous occupational surname indeed!

Do you know a Carter, Smith, Clark, Miller, Baker, Cook, Cartwright?

Once you start to collect names, you will be alert to new and unusual ones. Don't worry if you can find only a few to begin with. You have years to fill up your autograph book as you cross paths with new people and their names.

18 *Someday You May Name the Baby*

Someday you may be naming a brand-new baby. What names do you like? Do you want to stay with the fine old traditional ones? Or do you want to give your child one of the exotic, foreign names that are spilling over into our hemisphere?

There are many ways to create a new name, too. Here are some of them:

1. Take a word that has a special meaning for you and change the letters around until you have something that pleases you. If you love the ocean, you can make up the name Neaco (from the letters of "ocean") for a boy, Cenoa for a girl (again, "ocean" scrambled up).

2. Turn the letters of a favorite person around or change the spelling slightly. Lorna becomes Anrol; Sandra, Sandria.

3. Take a boy's name and switch it to a girl's and vice versa. Joni for John, Corinne to Corey.

4. Experiment! Today, almost anything goes. You aren't restricted to the traditional names. Just remember that you want the name to be one your child will like.

When you name your baby, keep in mind your last name. If the baby is a girl, the last name may change. But if the baby is a boy, the last name will probably always be your child's last name, too. If you have a long surname like Husslemeyer, you might want a short first name. Benjamin Husslemeyer is a pretty big mouthful. John Husslemeyer sounds better. It also works the other way around. A short last name needs a long given one. Jane Jones falls flat; Rebecca Jones is nicely balanced.

English parents in the early to mid-nineteenth century often gave young ones a hefty first name to make up for a skimpy last name. But their names were a bit fanciful—and more than a bit impossible. Abishag, Jeberechiah, Philadelphia, and Brittanica were very large names to give little people.

Names can be big in other ways. You can give your child the name of someone you want him or her to live up to. It might be the name of a writer, a doctor, or a scientist. It could be the name of a wise man from the pages of ancient history.

John *Aristotle* Phillips, a recent college student, has such a name. Aristotle was a classical philosopher whose wisdom was sought by all within traveling distance of him.

John's parents did not give him this inspiring middle name, but he has assumed it as a result of a fascinating series of events:

John owes his illustrious middle name to the FBI. But that is the *end* of the story. The beginning is that John Phillips designed his own atomic bomb—at the age of twenty-one. When he was a Princeton University student, Phillips worked up drawings of this lethal weapon for a classroom project. His "homework" made the newspapers and he became an instant celebrity.

He was also in danger. Even though he based the formulas for his bomb on nonsecret, published information, foreign agents tried to reach him. Strangers followed him across the campus. The FBI stepped in, anxious about his safety. They used the code name Aristotle to contact him. Not a bad choice. Surely the young student was an Aristotle to have figured out the makeup of the bomb. He also showed the ancient philosopher's wisdom when he said that he made the drawings to show how easy it was to develop the deadly weapon. He wanted the United States Government to be aware that a top secret weapon was not so secret after all.

There are other motivations behind naming. Impulse can often play a major role. A person may be so inspired by an event or experience that he or she designs the child's name around the happening.

Mrs. Douongdarra Keohavong of Laos did just that. She gave birth to her baby on an Air France Boeing 747 jet plane, 26,060 feet in the air. The passengers were delighted to be part of the great event and contributed to a fund for the baby. Mrs. Keoha-

vong, pleased by the attention, allowed the pilot to name the baby. Pilot Ernest Cleran suggested Francine in honor of his native country, France.

In Alexandria, Egypt, a baby was born just after the 1978 Israeli-Egyptian peace agreement orchestrated by President Carter. His last names were Mohammed Abdel Salam Hassan. His first name? Carter.

Your name is something special. It's a gift. Your parents gave you your first name. They passed on their last name. They would like you to appreciate the first and uphold the last. Your name is given to you in trust. By your actions you can make it a good name now, a great name later.

Your name, first or last, may be the nicest thing you will give a son or daughter someday.

DICTIONARY OF FIRST NAMES

BOYS

AARON light, mountain. Hebrew. Brother of Moses.

ABRAHAM father of a multitude. Hebrew. Abe Lincoln, sixteenth President.

ADAM man, red earth. Hebrew. According to the Bible, the first man.

ALAN handsome (Gaelic), harmony (Celtic). Also spelled Allan, Allen.

ALBERT noble, illustrious. German. Albert Schweitzer, missionary and musician.

ALEXANDER protector of men. Greek. Sir Alexander Fleming, discoverer of penicillin.

ALFRED elf-counsel. Anglo-Saxon. Elves, to the Anglo-Saxons, were powerful nature spirits.

ANDREW manly, strong, courageous. Greek. England's Prince Andrew made the name popular.

ANTHONY praiseworthy, priceless. Latin. Nickname: Tony.

ARNOLD strong as an eagle. German.

ARTHUR strong as a rock. Irish. King Arthur, a British king, leader of the Knights of the Round Table.

BARNARD, BERNARD stern bear. German. Nickname: Bernie.

BARRY good marksman. Celtic.

BENJAMIN son of the right hand. Hebrew. Nickname: Ben. Ben Franklin, statesman.

BERT noble, illustrious. German. From ALBERT. Bert, the chimney sweep in *Mary Poppins.*

BRADLEY broad lea or meadow. Anglo-Saxon.

BRIAN, BRYAN strength. Celtic. Bryan Donkin, inventor of method for preserving food in tins.

BRUCE brushwood thicket. Scottish. Originally the name of a French castle.

BURTON hill town, borough town. English.

BYRON   bear   (Anglo-Saxon), the cottage (English place-name).

CALVIN   the bald. Latin. John Calvin, sixteenth-century Protestant Reformer.

CARY, CAREY   fort, stony island. English and Welsh.

CHAD   defender. Celtic.

CHARLES   a man, strong. German, through Latin and French. Charles Dickens, writer; Prince Charles, heir to the British throne.

CHRISTOPHER   Christ bearer. Greek. Patron saint of travelers.

CHUCK   a man, strong. German. From CHARLES. Chuck Bednarik, football player.

CLARK   learned, a priest or scholar. Latin. Clark Kent, mild-mannered reporter (Superman).

CLAYTON   farm or town on clay site. English.

CLIFFORD   river crossing near the cliff. English. Nickname: Cliff.

CLINTON   hill farm or town. English.

COLIN   young hound, youth (Celtic), victory of the people (Greek). A pet name for NICHOLAS.

CONRAD   bold counsel. German.

CORY, COREY   ravine. Scottish place-name.

CRAIG   steep, rugged rock. Celtic.

CROSBY   near the crossroad. English place-name.

DALE   valley. English.

DANIEL   God is my judge. Hebrew. The Biblical Daniel was ·delivered from the lions' den.

DARRELL, DARRYL   beloved. Anglo-Saxon.

DAVID   beloved. Hebrew. The Biblical David who fought Goliath; the fictional David Copperfield.

DENNIS   of Dionysus, the Greek god of vegetation and wine. Greek and Old French.

DEREK   people-ruler. A Dutch abbreviation of German Theodoric.

DONALD   world-ruler. Gaelic. The MacDonalds are an ancient Scottish clan.

DOUGLAS   dark water. Scottish. General Douglas MacArthur.

DWIGHT   the white, the fair. English. General Dwight D. Eisenhower, thirty-fourth President.

EARL   nobleman. Anglo-Saxon.

EDGAR   happy warrior. Anglo-Saxon. Edgar Bergen, ventriloquist.

EDMUND   guardian of prosperity. Anglo-Saxon. Nickname: Ned. Sir Edmund Hillary climbed Mt. Everest.

EDWARD   defender of prosperity. Anglo-Saxon. Nickname: Ned.

EDWIN rich friend. Anglo-Saxon.

ERIC ruler. Norse. Early hero.

ERNEST sincerity, vigor. German. Nickname: Ernie.

EUGENE well-born, born lucky, noble. Greek.

FLOYD gray, dark-complexioned. Welsh. Floyd Patterson, boxer.

FRANCIS Frenchman, free. Latin. Francis Scott Key, composer of "The Star-spangled Banner."

FRANKLIN a middle-class landowner. English. Franklin D. Roosevelt, thirty-second President.

FREDERICK peace-ruler. German.

GARY powerful with the spear. Anglo-Saxon.

GENE well-born. Greek. From EUGENE.

GEOFFREY, JEFFREY land-peace. German. Lord Jeffrey Amherst, patron of Amherst College.

GEORGE farmer. Greek. First President's first name.

GERALD spear-force. German. Nicknames: Gerry and Jerry.

GILBERT bright pledge. German.

GLEN, GLENN valley. Celtic. As a last name, Glenn. John Glenn, first American to orbit the earth in space.

GORDON triangular hill. Anglo-Saxon.

GREGORY watchman. Greek. Pope Gregory XIII established the Gregorian calendar, which we now use.

GUS majestic. Latin. Short form of Augustus.

HANK home-ruler. German. From HENRY.

HAROLD army-power. Anglo-Saxon. Nicknames: Hal, Harry.

HARRY Older form of HENRY. Also nickname for HENRY or HAROLD.

HARVEY battle-worthy. Breton. Harvey, the imaginary rabbit of the stage.

HENRY home-ruler. German. Henry Hudson, English navigator. Nickname: Harry.

HERBERT bright-army. German. Nicknames: Bert and Herb.

HERMAN army-man. German. Herman Melville, author of *Moby Dick.*

HOWARD strong mind, watchman. German. Nickname: Howie.

HUGH mind, thought. German.

IAN the Lord is gracious. Hebrew. A Gaelic form of JOHN.

IRVIN beautiful, handsome. Gaelic.

ISAAC laughter. Hebrew. Isaac

Newton, discoverer of laws of motion and gravity.

JACK   the Lord is gracious. Hebrew. From JOHN.

JAMES   the supplanter. Hebrew. A form of Jacob. In Scotland, spelled Jamie.

JASON   healer. Greek. The legendary hero Jason sought the Golden Fleece.

JAY   Jay, the name of a bird.

JEROME   sacred name. Greek. Nickname: Jerry.

JOHN   the Lord is gracious. Hebrew. Johnny Appleseed (John Chapman), planter of apple trees across America.

JONATHAN   gift of the Lord. Hebrew. Nickname: Jon.

JOSEPH   he will add. Hebrew.

JOSHUA   the Lord saves. Hebrew. Biblical Joshua, leader of the Israelites.

JUSTIN   just. Latin. Roman emperor Justinian, the lawgiver.

KEITH   wood, windy place. Scottish. Keith Miller, famous Australian cricketer.

KENNETH   handsome by birth. Celtic. The first king of Scotland.

KEVIN   handsome, kind. Irish. Kevin Barry died to save the Irish Republic in 1916.

KIRK   church. Scottish. Also spelled Kirke.

KURT   bold counsel. German. From CONRAD.

LAWRENCE, LAURENCE   laurel tree. Latin. Nickname: Larry.

LEE   lea or meadow. Anglo-Saxon. Sometimes a nickname for Leonard.

LELAND   meadowland. English place-name.

LEROY   the king. French. Nickname: Roy.

LESTER   camp of legion. From Leicester, a place-name. Latin. Nickname: Les.

LLOYD   gray, dark-complexioned. Welsh.

LOUIS, LEWIS   famous in battle. German and French.

LUTHER   illustrious warrior. German. Martin Luther, leader of the Protestant Reformation; Martin Luther King, Jr., civil rights leader.

MALCOLM   servant of St. Columba. Scottish. Sir Malcolm Campbell, driver of the first automobile to exceed 300 miles per hour.

MARK   warlike. Latin. From the Roman war-god, Mars.

MARSHALL   high officer or official. French.

MARTIN   of Mars, warlike. Latin.

MARVIN   beautiful sea. Celtic. Nickname: Marv.

MATTHEW   gift of the Lord. Hebrew. Matthew the apostle, a tax collector before he followed Christ.

MICHAEL who is like God? Hebrew. Nickname: Mickey.

MILTON mill town or farm. English place-name.

MONROE mouth of the Roe River. Celtic. The Roe River is in Ireland.

MORRIS Moorish, dark. French and Latin. Nickname: Morrie.

MURRAY seaside settlement. Gaelic. Scottish place-name.

NATHANIEL gift of God. Hebrew. Nickname: Nate.

NED Nickname for EDWARD or EDMUND.

NEIL, NEAL chief (Irish), dark (Latin).

NELSON son of NEIL.

NICHOLAS victory of the people. Greek. Santa Claus is Dutch for St. Nicholas.

OWEN youth. Welsh.

PATRICK of noble birth. Latin. Legend says St. Patrick rid Ireland of snakes.

PAUL small. Latin. Paul Revere, famous midnight rider.

PETER rock. Greek. St. Peter Claver, seventeenth-century helper of black slaves.

PHILIP lover of horses. Greek. Prince Philip, consort of Queen Elizabeth II of England.

RALPH wolf-counsel. Anglo-Saxon.

RANDOLPH shield-wolf. Anglo-Saxon. Variation of Randall.

RAYMOND counsel-protection. German. Nickname: Ray.

REGINALD power-might. German. A favorite warrior name.

RICHARD strong ruler. German.

ROBERT bright fame. Anglo-Saxon. Robert Louis Stevenson, author of *Treasure Island.*

RODNEY reed island. Anglo-Saxon. Nickname: Roddy.

ROGER fame-spear. German. The Jolly Roger, a pirate flag.

ROLAND famous land. German. A famous French warrior.

RONALD power-might. Scottish version of REGINALD.

ROSCOE swift horse. Anglo-Saxon.

RUDOLPH, RUDOLF famous wolf. German.

SAMUEL "name of God." Hebrew. Samuel Morse, inventor of a telegraph code.

SCOTT native of Scotland. English. Often a last name.

SEAN the Lord is gracious. Hebrew. Irish form of JOHN.

SHAWN the Lord is gracious. Hebrew. A different spelling of SEAN.

SIDNEY, SYDNEY of St. Denis. French with English changes.

STANLEY stony field. English place-name.

STEPHEN, STEVEN crown, wreath. Greek.

SYLVESTER of the woods. Latin.

TED God's gift. Greek. From THEODORE.

THEODORE God's gift. Greek. Nickname: Teddy.

THOMAS twin. Aramaic (the language of Palestine at the time of Jesus).

TIMOTHY honoring God. Greek.

TODD fox. Scottish. Also a last name.

TONY praiseworthy, priceless. Latin. From ANTHONY.

TYRONE land of Owen. Irish.

VICTOR conqueror. Latin. The fictional Frankenstein's first name!

VINCENT conquering. Latin. St. Vincent, seventeenth-century French priest, caretaker of lost children.

WALTER powerful warrior. German. Nickname: Walt.

WARD guard. German.

WARREN protector. German. Warren Beatty, movie actor.

WAYNE maker of wagons. Short form of Wainwright. Anglo-Saxon.

WESLEY west field. Anglo-Saxon.

WHITNEY fair water. English place-name.

WILBERT, WILBUR bright pledge. German. From GILBERT.

WILL will-helmet. German. From WILLIAM. Will Rogers, actor and humorist.

WILLIAM will-helmet, protector. From the two Old German words *vilja* and *helma*. Nickname: Bill.

WINSTON friend-stone, firm friend. Anglo-Saxon. Sir Winston Churchill, British leader during World War II.

ZEKE God strengthens. Hebrew. Nickname for Ezekiel.

DICTIONARY OF FIRST NAMES

GIRLS

ABIGAIL source of joy. Hebrew. "Dear Abby" is an Abigail.

AGNES pure. Greek. St. Agnes, a patron saint of young girls.

ALICE nobility (German), truth (Greek). Alice in *Alice's Adventures in Wonderland.*

AMANDA lovable. From Latin *amare* (to love).

AMY the beloved. French. Amy Carter, daughter of the thirty-ninth President.

ANDREA strong, courageous. Greek. Feminine of ANDREW. Name first appeared in England in 1617.

ANGELA heavenly messenger, angel. Greek.

ANITA full of grace, mercy. Hebrew. A pet name for ANN.

ANN, ANNE full of grace, mercy. Hebrew. Little Orphan Annie, comic-strip character.

AUDREY strong, noble. From Old English *Aethelthryth.*

BARBARA mysterious stranger. Greek. St. Barbara was so beautiful her father kept her locked in a tower.

BEATRICE bringer of joy. Latin. Variation of Beatrix. Beatrix Potter, famous author.

BELLA oath of God. Hebrew. From ISABEL. Bella Abzug, feminist.

BERNICE bringer of victory. Greek.

BERTHA shining, bright. German. Nickname: Birdie.

BETH oath of God. Hebrew. From ELIZABETH.

BETSY oath of God. Hebrew. From ELIZABETH. Betsy Ross, famous Philadelphian.

BETTY oath of God. Hebrew. From ELIZABETH. Also spelled Bette. Betty Friedan, women's movement leader.

BEVERLY beaver meadow. English. Popular boy's name in England.

BONNIE sweet and good. Latin and Gaelic.

BRENDA fiery, aflame. Norse.

CANDACE Title of Ethiopian queens. Nickname: Candy.

CARLA one who is strong. German. See CHARLES. Also Karla.

CAROL joyous song. Also Carole, Caryl.

CAROLINE one who is strong. German. See CHARLES. Caroline of Monaco and Caroline Kennedy.

CATHERINE, CATHARINE pure. Greek. Nicknames: Kate, Kit, Kitty.

CHARLOTTE one who is strong. German. See CHARLES.

CHERYL dear, beloved. French.

CHRISTINA, CHRISTINE a Christian. Greek and Latin. Nickname: Tina.

CHRISTY a Christian. Greek and Latin. From CHRISTINA.

CLAIRE bright, illustrious. Latin and French.

CONSTANCE unchanging. Latin. Nickname: Connie.

CORA maiden. Greek. Coretta King

CYNTHIA from Mt. Cynthus. A title of the Greek moon-goddess Artemis. Nickname: Cindy.

DANIELLE God is my judge. Hebrew. Feminine of DANIEL.

DAWN the break of day. English.

DEBORAH bee. Hebrew. The bee symbolized royal power in ancient Egypt. Nicknames: Debby, Deb.

DEIRDRE the sorrowful. Irish. Nickname: Dee Dee.

DIANA, DIANE Roman moon-goddess. Diana was also the goddess of hunting and protector of wild animals.

DOLORES sorrows. Short for María de Dolores, Our Lady of Sorrows. Spanish.

DONNA Italian for lady.

DORIS bountiful. Greek. In mythology, Doris was the mother of fifty sea nymphs!

DOROTHY God's gift. Greek. Dorothy in The Wonderful Wizard of Oz. Nicknames: Dolly, Dotty.

EDITH prosperous war. From Anglo-Saxon Eadgyth.

EDWINA rich friend. Anglo-Saxon. Nickname: Winnie.

ELAINE light, the bright one. Greek. Old French form of HELEN.

ELEANOR light, the bright one. Greek. From HELEN. Eleanor Roosevelt.

ELENA light, the bright one. Greek. From HELEN.

ELIZABETH, ELISABETH oath of God. Hebrew. St. Elizabeth remembered the poor.

ELLEN light, the bright one. Greek. From HELEN. Very well-known in Ireland.

EMILY industrious. Latin. Nickname: Emmy.

EMMA one who heals. German. Nickname: Emmy.

ERICA of royalty. Norse. Feminine of ERIC.

ERIN Ireland in Old Irish or Gaelic.

EUNICE happy victory. Greek.

EVE, EVA life, living. Hebrew

FAITH trusting, faithful. Once an English boy's name.

FELICIA happy. Latin. *Felices Navidades,* Merry Christmas in Spanish.

FLORENCE flowering, blooming. Latin. Nickname: Flossie. Florence Nightingale.

FRANCES free. Latin. Nickname: Franny.

GAIL source of joy. Hebrew. From ABIGAIL.

GAY merry, lighthearted.

GERALDINE ruler with a spear. The name Geraldine was originally given by a poet to Lady Elizabeth FitzGerald. Nickname: Gerry.

GERTRUDE spear-strength. German. Nickname: Trudy.

GILLIAN soft-haired, youthful. Latin. English form of Juliane.

GLORIA glory, fame. Latin.

GRACE grace, thanks. Latin. Grace Kelly of Philadelphia became Princess Grace of Monaco.

GRETCHEN pearl. Greek. Pet form of MARGARET.

GWENDOLYN white-browed. Welsh. Nickname: Wendy.

HARRIET mistress of the home. Feminine form of HENRY. Nickname: Hattie. Harriet Tubman, an escaped slave, helped other slaves escape during the Civil War.

HEATHER A plant or flower name. English.

HEIDI nobility. German. From the last syllable of Adelaide. The small heroine in Swiss tale by Johanna Spyri.

HELEN light, the bright one. Greek. Nickname: Nellie. Old King Cole was a British king whose daughter's name was Helen. Helen Keller, blind writer and humanitarian.

HOLLY holy, good luck. English. Girls born near Christmas are often called Holly.

INGRID Ing's ride. Ing was the Norse god of peace and prosperity. Ingrid Bergman, screen star.

IRENE peace. Greek. Nickname: Renie.

ISABEL oath of God. Hebrew. From ELIZABETH.

JACQUELINE the supplanter. Hebrew. From Jacques or JAMES. Nickname: Jackie. Jacqueline Onassis, President Kennedy's wife.

JANE the Lord is gracious. Hebrew. Feminine of JOHN. Jane Austen, writer; Jane Eyre, fictional heroine.

JANET   the Lord is gracious. Hebrew. From JANE.

JEAN   the Lord is gracious. Hebrew. Modern Scottish form of JANE or JOAN.

JENNIFER   fair lady, white-cheeked. From Guinevere. Welsh.

JESSICA   riches, grace of God. Probably Hebrew.

JILL   From JULIA or GILLIAN.

JOAN   the Lord is gracious. Hebrew. Feminine of JOHN. Joan of Arc.

JOANNE   the Lord is gracious. Hebrew. From JOHN.

JODI   A variation of JUDITH or JOAN.

JOY   joy. Short for Joyce.

JUANITA   the Lord is gracious. Hebrew. Spanish pet form of JOAN.

JUDITH   of Judah. Hebrew. Nickname: Judy.

JULIA   soft-haired, youthful. Latin. From Julius. July was named after the Roman emperor Julius Caesar.

JUNE   Name of the month.

KARA, CARA   beloved. From Italian cara (dear).

KAREN   pure. Greek. Danish form of KATHERINE.

KATE   pure. Greek. From KATHERINE.

KATHERINE   pure. Greek. A name of saints, queens, heroines.

KATHLEEN   pure. Greek. Irish form of KATHERINE.

KELLY   An Irish last name used as a first name.

KIM   chief. Probably Anglo-Saxon.

KIRSTEN   a Christian. Scandinavian.

KRISTEN   a Christian. English.

LAURA   the laurel. Latin. Laurel tree, favorite of the god Apollo.

LEE   meadow. Anglo-Saxon.

LESLIE   low meadow. Anglo-Saxon.

LIBBY   oath of God. Hebrew. From ELIZABETH.

LILLIAN   the lily. English. Variations: Lila, Lili.

LINDA   beautiful.   Spanish. Many spellings: Lindy, Lynda.

LISA   oath of God. Hebrew. From ELIZABETH.

LOIS   good, desirable. Greek.

LORI   From LAURA or LORRAINE.

LORRAINE   famous in battle. German and French.

LOUISE   famous in battle. German and French. Feminine of LOUIS.

LUCY   light. Latin. Lucille Ball, actress.

MABEL   amiable, loving. Latin.

MARCIA   of Mars. Latin. Feminine of MARK.

MARGARET   pearl. Greek. Nicknames: Meg, Maggie, Marge.

MARGO pearl. Greek. From MARGARET.

MARIA bitterness, wished-for child. Hebrew. Latin form of MARY.

MARIAN bitterness, wished-for child. Hebrew. From MARY.

MARIE bitterness, wished-for child. Hebrew. From MARY.

MARILYN bitterness, wished-for child. Hebrew. From MARY.

MARJORIE pearl. Greek. From MARGARET.

MARLENE A combination of MARY and Magdalene.

MARTHA lady. Aramaic. Martha Washington, the first President's wife.

MARY bitterness, wished-for child. From Hebrew MIRIAM. Mary, the mother of Jesus.

MAURA, MOIRA bitterness, wished-for child. Hebrew. From Máire and Moire, Irish forms of MARY.

MAUREEN bitterness, wished-for child. Hebrew. From Máirin, an Irish form of MARY.

MEG pearl. Greek. From MARGARET.

MELANIE dark. Greek. Popular in England.

MELISSA bee. Greek. Old favorite for nymphs and fairies. Nickname: Missy.

MICHELLE, MICHELE who is like God? Hebrew. Feminine of MICHAEL.

MILDRED mild power. From Old English *milde* (mild) and *thryth* (power).

MIMI bitterness, wished-for child. Hebrew. Pet form of MIRIAM or MARY.

MIRIAM bitterness, wished-for child. Hebrew. Sister of Moses.

MONICA adviser. Latin. Monica, the mother of St. Augustine.

NANCY full of grace, mercy. Hebrew. From ANN.

NATALIE birthday. Latin. The birthday of Christ, Christmas.

NICOLE victory of the people. Greek.

NINA full of grace, mercy. Hebrew. Pet form of ANN.

NORA light, the bright one. Greek. Shortened form of ELEANOR.

OLIVIA olive. Latin. The olive branch is a symbol of peace.

PAMELA loving, kind, beloved elf.

PATRICIA of the nobility. Latin. Nickname: Patsy.

PAULA little. Latin. Feminine of PAUL.

PEARL A jewel name. Sometimes a nickname for MARGARET.

PEG pearl. Greek. Nickname for MARGARET.

PENELOPE weaver. Greek. Nickname: Penny.

PHYLLIS green bough. Greek.

POLLY   bitterness, wished-for child. Hebrew. From MARY.

PRISCILLA   the ancient. Latin.

RACHEL   ewe, female sheep. Hebrew. Nickname: Shelley.

REBECCA   to bind, knotted cord, faithful wife. Hebrew. Becky Thatcher, fictional heroine of *The Adventures of Tom Sawyer*.

RITA   pearl. Greek. From MARGARET.

ROBERTA   of shining fame. Anglo-Saxon. Feminine of ROBERT.

ROBIN   of shining fame. Anglo-Saxon. From ROBERT.

ROSE   a rose.

RUTH   vision of beauty (Hebrew), compassion (English). Ruth, of the Bible, revered for her faithfulness.

SALLY   princess. Hebrew. Originally a nickname for SARA.

SANDRA   helper of mankind. Greek.

SARA, SARAH   princess. Hebrew.

SHANNON   An Irish place-name.

SHARON   of Sharon. Hebrew. Rose of Sharon, a plant.

SHEILA   dim-sighted. Irish form of Cecilia.

SHELLEY   meadow full of shells. Anglo-Saxon.

SHERI   beloved one. From French *chérie*.

SHIRLEY   district meadow. English. Shirley Temple, child actress.

SONIA   wisdom. Russian form of Sophia. Sonja Henie, ice skater.

STACEY   resurrection. Greek.

STEPHANIE   crown or garland. Greek.

SUSAN   lily. Hebrew.

SYLVIA   forest maiden. Latin.

TAMMY   palm tree. Hebrew. Tammy in *Tammy and the Bachelor*.

TANYA   Favorite Russian name. A short form of Tatiana.

TARA   tower. Irish.

TERRY, TERRI   harvester. Greek. From Teresa.

VALERIE   strong, healthy. Latin. From Valentine.

VANESSA   butterfly.   Greek. Nickname: Van.

VERA   true (Latin), faith (Russian).

VICTORIA   victory.   Latin. Queen Victoria.

VIRGINIA   maidenly,   pure. Latin. Virginia is a state, too.

VIVIAN   full of life. Latin.

WENDY   white-browed. Welsh. From GWENDOLYN. Wendy flies to Never-Never Land in *Peter Pan*.

WYNNE   the fair, the white. Celtic.

YOLANDA   violet. From Old French Violante.

YVONNE   yew wood, archer's

BIBLIOGRAPHY

Andersen, Christopher, *The Name Game*. Simon & Schuster, 1977.

Bander, Edward J., *Change of Name and Law of Names*. Oceana Publications, 1973.

Booklet for Women Who Wish to Determine Own Names After Marriage. Center for Woman's Own Name. Published in the U.S.A., 1974.

Boutell, Charles, *Boutell's Heraldry,* rev. by J. P. Brooke-Little. Frederick Warne & Co., 1970.

Browder, Sue, *The New Age Baby Name Book*. Warner Books, 1974.

Burton, Dorothy, *A New Treasury of Names for the Baby*. Prentice-Hall, 1961.

Dellquest, Augustus W., *These Names of Ours: A Book of Surnames*. Thomas Y. Crowell Co., 1938.

Dunkling, Leslie Alan, *First Names First*. Universe Books, 1977.

Foreign Versions, Variations and Diminutives of English Names. U.S. Government Printing Office, 1973.

Hilton, Suzanne, *Who Do You Think You Are? Digging for Your Family Roots*. Westminster Press, 1976.

Hughes, Charles James, *Is Thy Name Wart? The Origins of Some Curious and Other Surnames*. London: Phoenix House, 1965.

Kaganoff, Benzion C., *Dictionary of Jewish Names and Their History*. Schocken Books, 1977.

Kohl, Herbert, *Golden Boy as Anthony Cool: A Photo Essay on Naming and Graffiti*. Dial Press, 1972.

Lambert, Eloise, and Pei, Mario, *Our Names: Where They Come From and What They Mean*. Lothrop, Lee & Shepard Co., 1960.

Matthews, Constance Mary, *English Surnames*. Charles Scribner's Sons, 1967.

Nurnberg, Maxwell, and Rosenblum, Morris, *What to Name Your Baby: The Meaning and Story of Names*. Macmillan Co., Collier Books, 1962.

Ojigbo, A. Okion, ed., *Young and Black in Africa*. Random House, 1971 (Excerpt, F. Selormey, "My Sister Is Born").

Sleigh, Linwood, and Johnson, Charles, *The Book of Boys' Names.* Thomas Y. Crowell Co., 1962.

Sleigh, Linwood, and Johnson, Charles, *The Book of Girls' Names.* Thomas Y. Crowell Co., 1962.

"So You'd Like to Change Your Name," *New York Post,* Dec. 26, 1972, p. 8.

Spooner, Ella Brown, *Lullaby of Names.* Exposition Press, 1956.

Stannard, Una, *Married Women v. Husband's Names: The Case for Wives Who Keep Their Own Name.* Germain Books, 1973.

Sutton, Horace, "Game of the Name," *Saturday Review,* April 2, 1977.

Taggart, Jean, *Pet Names.* Scarecrow Press, 1962.

Tournier, Paul, *The Naming of Persons.* Harper & Row, 1974.

"What's in a Name," *The Christian Science Monitor,* Sept. 7, 1972, p. 1.

Withycombe, Elizabeth G., *The Oxford Dictionary of English Christian Names.* Oxford University Press, 1973.

ACKNOWLEDGMENTS

Many thanks to the short-named and long-named persons who contributed to this book:

To Virginia Day and the boys and girls at Germantown Academy, who provided a barometer of name preferences

To Burnap Post, for sharing the definitive Burnap Post speller!

To Bob Batchelder, for encouraging youngsters to start early in the autograph game and supplying ideas for collecting

To Bob Price, for sharing thoughts on going middle-nameless

To Carlos Baravalle, who supplied charming Spanish nicknames, including his own, Carlitos

To Dick Lee, built-in editor and kindly critic

To Rick, Barb, and Monica: their enthusiasm for name meanings was the inspiration behind this book

To everyone who has provided me with such name gems as June Jones, two-hundred-pound football player, and John Paul Jones, who sights sites instead of ships

INDEX

125